定点観測者としての通信社

戦争と平和
―― 80年の記憶 ――

A news agency as eyewitness

War and Peace
― 80 Years of Memories ―

公益財団法人 新聞通信調査会
Japan Press Research Institute

目次 / Contents

- 3 ── 開催に当たって
  Greeting from Photo Exhibition Organizer

図版　Plates

- 5 ── プロローグ：80年の時を経て
  Prologue : After 80 Years

- 17 ── 第1章：過信の果て
  Chapter 1 : The Consequences of Overconfidence

- 37 ── 第2章：「平和国家」の虚実
  Chapter 2 : The Illusions of a "Peaceful Nation"

- 77 ── 第3章：混迷の時代
  Chapter 3 : An Era of Turmoil

- 113 ── エピローグ：戦火の子どもたち
  Epilogue : Children of War

寄稿

- 124　「日本の記憶」と「世界の戦争」／小熊英二

- 126　途切れなき戦争、なし崩しの「平和」／西崎文子

凡例
・日付のない写真は日付が特定できなかったものである。
・クレジットの記載のない写真、グラフィックスは共同通信社提供。

報道写真展「戦争と平和―80年の記憶―」開催に当たって

　2024年のノーベル平和賞は、被爆者の立場から核兵器廃絶を訴えてきた日本原水爆被害者団体協議会（日本被団協）が受賞した。「原爆の父」と呼ばれる物理学者の苦悩と葛藤を描いた映画「オッペンハイマー」が日本で公開されたのも、奇しくも同じ年だった。終末時計がロシアによるウクライナへの核威嚇などで過去最短の「90秒」に迫る中、改めて核兵器を考えるきっかけになったのではないだろうか。

　同年8月15日の終戦の日、政府の全国戦没者追悼式には3000人を超える遺族が参列したが、うち戦後生まれが47％と過去最高だった。遺族の世代交代が進み、戦争の記憶は遠ざかりつつある。天皇陛下のお言葉にある「さきの大戦」は、米国にならって太平洋戦争と呼ぶのが一般的だが、アジア太平洋戦争という表記も目立つようになった。欧州を含めれば第2次世界大戦であり、日本は当時、大東亜戦争と呼んだ。

　戦争の呼称の問題は歴史認識にもつながる。太平洋戦争は、「玉砕」や「空襲」「原爆」などから、どうしても戦争の惨禍、被害者のイメージだけが前面に出がちだ。アジア太平洋戦争とすれば、抜け落ちていたアジア諸国への加害の事実に目を向けることができる。京都生まれの朴沙羅さん（社会学者）が24年秋、朝日新聞に書いていた「うんざりした『あの戦争』の平和教育」と題したコラムを思い出した。

　「8月ジャーナリズム」とは、「原爆の日」から「終戦の日」にかけて新聞やテレビなどが集中的に取り上げる戦争関連特集のことである。ともすれば戦争被害の記憶だけを取り上げ、自然災害のように戦争を描いて平和の重要性を強調するパターン化したメディアの姿勢を批判する人たちもいる。朴さんの考えもこれに近い。韓国に駐在経験のある筆者もかねて違和感を持っていた。

　25年は戦後80年の節目。この間、日本は幸いにも戦禍を被ることはなかった。しかし、世界では今もウクライナで、中東ガザで、悲惨な戦争、紛争が続いている。アジアでは戦後、朝鮮戦争、ベトナム戦争があった。日本の周辺では現在、北朝鮮が核開発を進め、台湾有事も取り沙汰される。そうした中で、平和の問題をもう一度考える契機になればと、今回の写真展を企画した。

　構成はプロローグ「80年の時を経て」に始まって、第1章「過信の果て」、第2章「『平和国家』の虚実」、第3章「混迷の時代」と続く。そしてエピローグ「戦火の子どもたち」まで、107枚の内外の写真で振り返った。写真展の開催に当たっては、今回も共同通信社の協力を得ました。定点観測者としての通信社についてもご理解いただければ幸いです。

公益財団法人 新聞通信調査会
理事長　西沢　豊

Greeting from Photo Exhibition Organizer

The 2024 Nobel Peace Prize was awarded to Nihon Hidankyo (Japan Confederation of A- and H-Bomb Sufferers Organizations) for their activism to abolish nuclear weapons from the perspective of victims and survivors. In a strange twist, this was the same year that the film Oppenheimer was released in Japan, portraying the anguish and conflicts of the physicist and "father of the atomic bomb", J. Robert Oppenheimer. Perhaps the doomsday clock, set to its shortest ever time of 90 seconds to midnight–reflecting Russia's nuclear threat against Ukraine has provided an opportunity to rethink nuclear weapons.

On the memorial day of the end of the war this year, August 15, over 3,000 relatives of the victims attended the government's Memorial Ceremony for the War Dead, of whom 47% were born after the war, a new high. Memories of the war are fading as the survivors' generation is replaced by new generations. While the Emperor referred to the war as Saki no taisen ("Last Great War"), it is mostly called "the Pacific War" in Japan as learnt from the United States, but in many places, it is now also known as the "Asia-Pacific War". When Europe is included, it is the Second World War, which in Japan in the 1940s, was called the "Greater East Asia War".

The issue of what we call the war is connected to historical knowledge. We have a tendency when it comes to the Pacific War to put images of disaster and victimhood to the forefront with phrases like "honorable death", "air raids" and "atomic bomb". By calling it the Asia-Pacific War, we can turn our focus to the reality of the damage we inflicted on the countries of Asia, which has been neglected in Japan. I am reminded of the column for the Asahi Shimbun newspaper written by Kyoto-born sociologist Sara Park from autumn 2024, entitled Unzarishita "ano senso" no heiwa kyoiku (Fed up with Peace education about "that war").

In newspapers and on TV, "August journalism" from Hiroshima Day (August 6) to End of the War Day (August 15) typically focuses on specials related to the war. Some people criticize the media tendency of emphasizing the importance of peace and portraying the war as something akin to natural disaster, where only the memories of war victims are covered. Park's perspective is close to this. As someone with experience living in South Korea, I have also long felt a sense of dissonance with this approach.

2025 will mark the 80th anniversary of the end of the war. Fortunately, Japan has not experienced war over this time. However, disastrous wars and conflicts continue around the world today from Ukraine to Gaza in the Middle East. In Asia, the postwar period brought the Korean War and the Vietnam War. Close to Japan, North Korea is developing nuclear weapons and the Taiwan situation is gaining urgency. In such a context, this photo exhibition was created as an opportunity to consider afresh the question of peace.

It is a retrospective of 107 photographs from Japan and abroad, structured to begin with the Prologue ("After 80 Years"), followed by Chapter 1 ("The Consequences of Overconfidence"), Chapter 2 ("The Illusions of a "Peaceful Nation"") and Chapter 3 ("An Era of Turmoil"), ending with the Epilogue, "Children of War". This exhibition is a collaboration with Kyodo News. We appreciate your understanding of news agency's role as an eyewitness.

Yutaka Nishizawa
Chairman
Japan Press Research Institute

プロローグ：80年の時を経て

Prologue：After 80 Years

プロローグ：80年の時を経て

東京の玄関口、JR東京駅
JR Tokyo Station, Gateway to Tokyo

2023（令和5）年7月31日、厳しい暑さの中、JR東京駅前を歩く家族連れ。1964年に東京―新大阪間で東海道新幹線が開業し、東京駅は2024年12月に開業110周年を迎えた。

Families walking by JR Tokyo Station amid intense summer heat, July 31, 2023. The Tokaido Shinkansen line between Tokyo and Shin-Osaka opened in 1964 and Tokyo Station marked its 110th anniversary in December 2024.

東京駅でたむろする孤児
Homeless children hanging around Tokyo Station

1946（昭和21）年8月、東京駅でたむろする孤児たち。48年2月に厚生省（現厚生労働省）が実施した調査では約12万3千人の戦災孤児や捨て子が確認された。当時は「浮浪児」と呼ばれて差別を受け、栄養失調などで亡くなる子もいた。

Orphaned children around Tokyo Station, August 1946. A survey led by the Ministry of Health and Welfare (present-day the Ministry of Health, Labour and Welfare) in February 1948 found that some 123,000 children had been orphaned or abandoned as a result of the war. These children were referred to as furo-ji ("street children") at the time and subjected to discrimination. Some of them even died of malnutrition.

空襲で焼け野原となった東京の下町
Downtown Tokyo burnt down after air raids

1945（昭和20）年10月10日、空襲で一面焼け野原となった東京の下町。中央を横切るのは隅田川で左が上流、右が河口側。橋は新大橋。隅田川の手前側は日本橋区（現中央区）。対岸は左側が本所区（現墨田区）、右側は深川区（現江東区）。（米通信隊撮影）

Downtown Tokyo was burnt down after devastating air raids on October 10, 1945. In the center of this photo, the Sumida River is flowing from left to right. The bridge is Shin-Ohashi Bridge. In front of Sumida River is Nihonbashi-ku (present-day Chuo Ward). Across the river to the left is Honjo-ku (Sumida Ward) and to the right is Fukagawa-ku (Koto Ward). Photo by US signal corps.

ビルが立ち並ぶ東京の下町
Buildings of Downtown Tokyo

2023（令和5）年11月5日、東京・日本橋付近の上空から見た下町一帯。都心部に多い超高層ビルは少ない。中央を横切るのは隅田川。中央左は両国国技館（緑の屋根）。左は東京スカイツリー。

Aerial shot taken from near Nihonbashi, looking over downtown Tokyo, November 5, 2023. There are fewer skyscrapers compared to other parts of the city. The Sumida River runs across the shot. At center left is the Ryogoku Kokugikan National Sumo Arena (with its distinctive green roof). Tokyo Skytree is on the left.

日本橋にカボチャ畑
Pumpkin field, Nihonbashi

1945(昭和20)年5月6日、空襲で焼け野原となった東京・日本橋で、食糧増産のためカボチャの種まきをする動員学徒。右後方のビルは日本橋高島屋。出征兵士の増加で農家の労働力が減少、食糧事情は急激に悪化した。戦争の拡大で労働力不足が深刻になると、中学以上の生徒や学生が軍需産業や食糧生産に動員され、45年には、授業停止による学徒勤労総動員体制が取られた。(同盟通信)

On May 6, 1945, students were mobilized to sow pumpkin seeds to increase food production in Nihonbashi, Tokyo, which had been burnt to the ground by air raids. The building at the right rear is "the Nihombashi Takashimaya". Due to many people being sent off to war as soldiers, the farming labor force was greatly reduced and food security deteriorated sharply. When the labor shortage became severe due to the expansion of the war, students in junior high school and above were mobilized to work for the munitions industry and food production. In 1945, all education beyond primary schools was suspended as all students were mobilized to join the labor force. (Domei News Agency)

日本橋を行くみこし行列
Mikoshi parade on the way to Nihonbashi

2024(令和6)年6月9日、東京・日本橋の高島屋本館前を行く夏祭りのみこし行列。高島屋本館は1933年に完成した歴史ある建物。戦災にも耐え、現在は国の重要文化財に指定されている。
On June 9, 2024, a mikoshi procession passed by "the Nihombashi Takashimaya" shopping center in Nihonbashi, Tokyo, during a summer festival. The department store, completed in 1933, is a historic building that survived the air raids and fires of the war. Today, it is designated as an important cultural property.

米海兵隊が横須賀に上陸
US Marine Corps ashore at Yokosuka

1945（昭和20）年8月30日、マッカーサー連合国軍最高司令官が神奈川県の厚木基地に降り立ったその日、米海兵隊が横須賀軍港に上陸した。31日にかけて横須賀地区に約1万7千人が上陸。日本全土に進駐した占領軍は、米軍や英連邦軍総計約40万人。中央奥の2本マストは記念艦「三笠」。（同盟通信）

On August 30, 1945, General Douglas MacArthur landed at Atsugi Air Base in Kanagawa Prefecture, and the US Marine Corps landed at Yokosuka Port on the same day. By August 31, some 17,000 US soldiers had arrived in the Yokosuka district. The Occupation expanded across Japan, involving US, British, and other Allied forces totaling some 400,000 troops. The two masts in the center rear are part of the memorial ship Mikasa. (Domei News Agency)

米海軍横須賀基地の原子力空母
Nuclear-powered aircraft carrier at Yokosuka U.S. naval base

2023（令和5）年9月28日、神奈川県横須賀市の米海軍横須賀基地に停泊する原子力空母ロナルド・レーガン（手前中央）。同空母は15年10月横須賀基地に入港、24年5月、約8年8カ月に及んだ任務を終え、同基地から出港した。乗組員は最大で約5千人。米海軍は計11隻の空母を保有するが、横須賀は唯一の海外母港。米軍によると、横須賀基地は米国外に展開する最大の海軍施設で、日米の計2万6千人以上が働いたり、生活したりしている。右上は横須賀市街。

On September 28, 2023, the USS Ronald Reagan, a nuclear-powered aircraft carrier, docked at Yokosuka US Naval Base, Yokosuka, Kanagawa Prefecture (center, foreground). The aircraft carrier first deployed to the port in October 2015 and left the base in May 2024 after completing some eight years and eight months of service. The USS Ronald Regan can accommodate a crew of up to 5,000. The US Navy possesses a total of 11 aircraft carriers, and Yokosuka is their only foreign homeport. According to the US military, Yokosuka is the largest US naval base outside of US, with over 26,000 American and Japanese workers and residents. Yokosuka City can be seen above on the right.

浦上天主堂で祈りをささげる
Prayers offered at Urakami Cathedral

2023（令和5）年8月9日、長崎市の浦上天主堂で開かれたミサで、原爆がさく裂した時刻に合わせて祈りをささげる参列者。かつての天主堂は原爆でほぼ全壊し、戦後しばらく、一部残った壁などの遺構を被爆の象徴として保存するか、解体して再建するかで議論になったが、最終的に撤去された。信徒たちは跡地に建てられた木造の仮設教会を使用した。現在のコンクリート製の天主堂は1959年に再建された。

On August 9, 2023, a mass was held at Urakami Cathedral in Nagasaki, with attendees praying to commemorate the exact time of the atomic blast. The former cathedral was almost completely destroyed. For some time after the war, there was a discussion about whether the remnants of walls should be left as symbols of the bombing or if the building should be demolished and rebuilt. Ultimately, the site was cleared, and a temporary wooden cathedral was built for worshippers. The concrete cathedral seen today was built in 1959.

倒壊した浦上天主堂跡で祈り
Prayers at the ruins of Urakami Cathedral

1946（昭和21）年8月、前年の8月に長崎に投下された原子爆弾で倒壊したカトリック教会「浦上天主堂」跡で祈りをささげる信徒たち。浦上地区には多くのカトリック信徒が暮らし、同地区の信徒約1万2千人のうち、8千人以上が45年末までに犠牲になったとされる。

In August 1946, Catholics gathered to pray at the ruins of the Urakami Cathedral, which had been destroyed when the atomic bomb was dropped on Nagasaki a year earlier. The Urakami district was home to some 12,000 Catholics, and over 8,000 of them were dead by the end of 1945.

第1章：過信の果て

　明治維新以来アジア諸国に先駆けて近代化を達成した日本は富国強兵に邁進し、アジア支配の野望を膨らませた。その結果米欧各国の疑念と反発を呼ぶことになった。西欧植民地支配からの解放を勝ち取り、アジア諸民族が共に繁栄するとうたった「大東亜共栄圏」はその理想とは裏腹に中国大陸と東南アジア、太平洋での泥沼の戦争へと自らを追いやった。

　日本と同じく近代化と帝国主義化に後れを取ったドイツ、イタリアと結んだ三国同盟（1940年）は理念や展望を欠き、国際的孤立を自ら招く決定的な国策の誤りの一例だった。ドイツ、イタリアが欧州で侵攻を始めると、日本は圧倒的な国力差をあえて無視して対米戦争に突入した。厳しい経済封鎖に対し、機先を制した電撃的な軍事作戦によって事態を打開できるという過信と根拠のない期待を背景とした愚挙に他ならなかった。

　それは日本外交の敗北であり、正しい情報から隔絶された国民の熱狂と軍部の専横に政治とメディアがなすすべなく従った結果でもあった。その報いは310万人の国民とアジア全体で2000万人が犠牲になったとされる惨禍として降りかかった。戦局の決定的悪化と敗戦が誰の目にも明らかとなってからも、政府と軍は判断と責任を放棄し被害をいたずらに拡大させ続けた。犠牲者のほとんどは終戦までの約1年間に集中した。

Chapter 1 : The Consequences of Overconfidence

After the Meiji Restoration, Japan pursued modernization and regional dominance, provoking Western backlash. The "Greater East Asia Co-Prosperity Sphere" led to wars across Asia and the Pacific.

The Tripartite Pact w th Germany and Italy (1940) lacked clear vision and deepened Japan's international isolation. Ignoring vast disparities in power, Japan entered war with the United States, driven by overconfidence and the unfounded belief that preemptive military action could counter economic blockades.

This failure, driven by unchecked military dominance, cost 3.1 million Japanese lives and 20 million lives across Asia were lost. Even as defeat became clear, the government and military prolonged devastation, with most casualties in the war's final year.

盧溝橋付近の日本軍部隊
Japanese Army troops near Marco Polo Bridge

1937（昭和12）年7月、北京郊外の盧溝橋付近に待機する日本軍部隊。日本軍は31年、奉天（現瀋陽）近郊の柳条湖で鉄道の線路を爆破し、それを口実に軍事行動を起こした。32年、かいらいの「満州国」を中国東北部に建国。37年の盧溝橋事件を発端に、日中戦争に突入した。（クレジット不明）

Imperial Japanese Army troops gathered for battle near the Marco Polo Bridge on the outskirts of Beijing, July 1937. In 1931, Japanese troops set off an explosion on a railway line at Liutiao Lake near Mukden (present-day Shenyang) and used it as a pretext for military action. In 1932, the puppet state of Manchukuo was founded in northeast China. The Marco Polo Bridge incident of 1937 precipitated the outbreak of Sino-Japanese War. (Credit: unknown)

日独伊三国同盟締結の祝賀会
Celebration of the signing of the Tripartite Pact between Japan, Germany, and Italy

1940（昭和15）年9月27日、東京の外相官邸で日独伊三国同盟締結を記念して開かれた祝賀会で、ドイツ、イタリアの大使らと乾杯する松岡洋右外相（右から4人目）、東条英機陸相（中央）ら。日中戦争開始により米国との関係は悪化していたが、三国同盟締結や、フランス領インドシナ南部（現ベトナム南部）への日本軍進駐により41年8月、米国は対日石油輸出を全面禁止。日米の対立が深刻化した。（同盟通信）

On September 27, 1940, celebrating the signing of the Tripartite Pact between Japan, Germany, and Italy, a reception was held at the Foreign Minister's official residence in Tokyo. The event was attended by Yosuke Matsuoka, Japanese Minister of Foreign Affairs(4th from R), Hideki Tojo, Minister of War(C), the German and Italian ambassadors. Relations with the United States had worsened since the outbreak of the Sino-Japanese War. In August 1941, the US banned all oil exports to Japan due to the signing of the Tripartite Pact and the Japanese invasion of French Indochina (present-day southern Viet Nam). The rift between the US and Japan worsened. (Domei News Agency)

ハワイ真珠湾を日本軍が攻撃
Japanese Army Attack on Pearl Harbor

1941（昭和16）年12月7日（日本時間8日）、日本海軍航空部隊による米ハワイ・オアフ島の真珠湾攻撃で炎上する米戦艦ウェストバージニアと水兵の救助に向かう船艇。米艦隊の被害は甚大で、民間人を含む約2400人が死亡。同じ日に陸軍は英領マレー半島に侵攻し、米英など連合国との太平洋戦争が始まった。（ロイター）

On December 7, 1941 (December 8, Japan time), the USS West Virginia was in flames after the Imperial Japanese Navy Air Service attacked Pearl Harbor, Oahu, Hawaii, and boats were sent to rescue sailors. The US naval fleet suffered enormous damage and some 2,400 people lost their lives, including civilians. On the same day, the Japanese Army invaded British Malaya, triggering the Pacific War against the US, Britain, and their Allies. (Reuters)

かっぽう着姿で軍事教練
Women in aprons receive military training

1942（昭和17）年1月28日、太平洋戦争が始まって間もない頃、かっぽう着姿の女性たちが銃を担いで行われた軍事教練。国家総動員体制が取られると国民生活の全てが戦時一色となった。学校や地域で派遣将校や国防婦人会などを中心に「銃後の守り」が強要され、竹やり戦闘訓練やバケツリレーの防火演習が盛んに行われた。（同盟通信）

On January 28, 1942, women dressed in kappogi (coverall aprons often worn over kimono) and holding guns received military training soon after the outbreak of the Pacific War. With the implementation of the National Mobilization System, signs of war were everywhere in the lives of all citizens. Military officers and the Women's Association for National Defense were dispatched to schools and communities to enforce the need to "protect the home front", promoting active participation of citizens in combat training using bamboo spears and bucket relay fire drills. (Domei News Agency)

出撃前の特攻隊員ら
Kamikaze pilots before departure

1944（昭和19）年12月、飛行服に身を包んだ特攻隊員ら。特攻隊は戦況が悪化した戦争末期、爆弾を装着した航空機や潜水艇で連合国軍の艦船に体当たりするために編成された部隊。生還を前提としない攻撃だった。撮影場所不明。（同盟通信）

Kamikaze Tokkotai (special attack unit) members dressed in flight uniform, December 1944. These units were organized toward the end of the war as Japan's situation deteriorated. They used aircraft and submarines equipped with explosives, which made suicide attacks against Allied ships. It was expected that no kamikaze pilot would survive such an attack. Location unknown. (Domei News Agency)

日本軍がビルマの油田を占領
Japanese Army captures Burmese oil field

1942(昭和17)年4月、ビルマ(現ミャンマー)のラングーン(現ヤンゴン)占領後に北上、イラワジ川沿いのエナンジョン油田を占領した日本軍。(同盟通信)

April 1942 – Following the occupation of Rangoon (present-day Yangon), Burma (present-day Myanmar), the Japanese Army advanced north to seize the Yenangyaung oil field on the Irrawaddy River. (Domei News Agency)

東京帝大で学徒出陣の壮行会
Send-off ceremony for students going to war at Tokyo Imperial University

1943(昭和18)年11月12日、東京帝国大学(現東京大)で学徒出陣の「全学壮行会」の後、安田講堂前を行進する学生たち。戦局が悪化するまでは、大学、旧制高校、専門学校などの学生は26歳まで徴兵が猶予されていた。43年、兵力不足を補うため徴兵猶予を停止。法文系を中心に20歳以上の学徒が休学扱いで兵役に就いた。学徒兵の総数は10万人以上とされる。(同盟通信)

Students march in front of Yasuda Auditorium following a "university-wide send-off ceremony" for students mobilized to the military frontline, Tokyo Imperial University (present-day University of Tokyo), November 12, 1943. Before the situation deteriorated for Japan, high school and university students, as well as vocational school students, had conscription deferred until the age of 26. However, in 1943, deferments were suspended due to troop shortages. Students aged 20 and above, particularly those studying law and the humanities, were pressed into service on leave of absence. The number of student soldiers likely exceeded 100,000. (Domei News Agency)

上野駅から疎開先へ
From Ueno Station to countryside refuges

1944（昭和19）年6月17日、東京・上野駅から疎開先の福島県に向かう東京都牛込区（現新宿区）の鶴巻国民学校の児童ら。戦況悪化を受けて東京都が「戦時疎開学園」を設置、保護者の要望に応え一部児童の疎開を実施した。8月4日には、政府の決定による大都市などから地方への40万人以上の学童集団疎開が始まった。（同盟通信）

Children from Tsurumaki Elementary School in Ushigome-ku (present-day Shinjuku Ward), Tokyo made their way from Ueno Station to refuge in Fukushima Prefecture, June 17, 1944. Due to the worsening war situation, the Tokyo Metropolitan Government established "war evacuation schools" and some children were evacuated upon their parents' or guardians' request. Starting from August 4, following a directive by the national government, over 400,000 children from major cities were evacuated in large groups to the countryside. (Domei News Agency)

サイパンの日本人の女性と子ども
Japanese women and children in Saipan

1944(昭和19)年7月、北マリアナ諸島サイパン島で、米軍によって集められた日本人の女性と子ども。米軍は6月にサイパンに上陸、日本軍は部隊全員の死を覚悟した「玉砕戦」を展開、民間人と合わせ約5万人が死亡したとされる。陥落後、隣のテニアン島とともに日本本土を空襲する米軍機の拠点となった。(ACME)

Japanese women and children gathered by US soldiers on Saipan, Northern Mariana Islands, July 1944. US forces had landed on Saipan in June, to be met with Gyokusaisen (honorable suicide battle) by Japanese troops. The total deaths numbered approximately 50,000 including civilians. After the fall of Saipan, the island and its neighboring Tinian became bases from which US aircraft conducted air raids over the Japanese mainland. (ACME)

昭和天皇が大空襲の被災地域視察
Emperor Hirohito visits the district struck by Great Tokyo air raid

1945(昭和20)年3月18日、東京大空襲で焼け野原となった深川の富岡八幡宮境内などを視察する昭和天皇。10日未明、米軍のB29爆撃機約300機が現在の江東区、墨田区、台東区などを中心に約2時間半にわたり焼夷弾を集中的に投下。10万人以上が犠牲になったとされる。軍施設や軍需工場が主な標的ではなく、市民が多く暮らす市街地全体を狙った無差別爆撃だった。(同盟通信)

On March 18, 1945, Emperor Hirohito visited the Tomioka Hachiman Shrine in Fukagawa, a district that had been devastated by the Great Tokyo air raid. In the pre-dawn of March 10, around 300 US B-29 Superfortress heavy bombers dropped incendiary bombs targeting the area of Koto Ward, Sumida Ward and Taito Ward for about two and a half hours. Over 100,000 people were killed. Rather than military installations or munitions factories, it was an indiscriminate attack targeting residential areas home to millions of people. (Domei News Agency)

沖縄本島に向けロケット弾
Rocket launched toward the Okinawa's main island

1945（昭和20）年、沖縄本島への上陸作戦で、日本軍の拠点に向けて米海軍の中型揚陸艦から発射されるロケット弾。米軍は3月下旬から連日艦砲射撃を実施。4月1日に本島の読谷村などに上陸、住民を巻き込んだ激しい地上戦を展開した。（米海軍公式写真）

In 1945, a rocket was fired from a Landing Ship Medium, an amphibious assault ship of the US Navy, towards the Japanese Army base during its landing operation on the main island of Okinawa. The US Navy carried out gunfire support for several days at the end of March. On April 1, US troops landed at Yomitan Village, resulting in fierce battles involving local civilians. (US Navy official photograph)

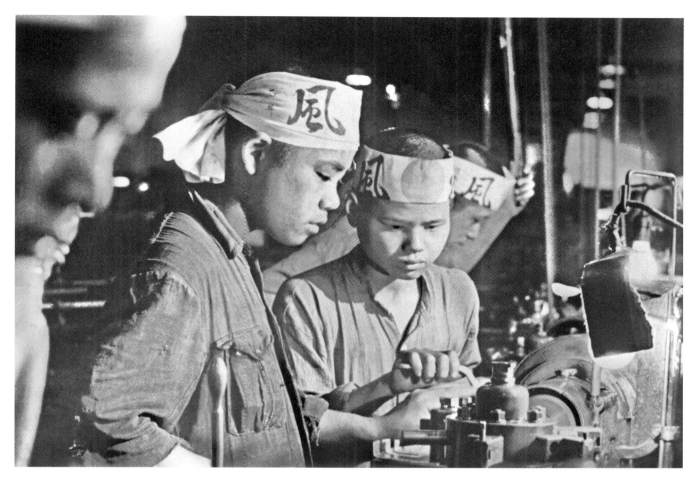

沖縄の軍需工場の少年
Boy at a munitions factory, Okinawa

1945(昭和20)年、沖縄の軍需工場で働く少年。沖縄での戦闘は45年3月26日、米軍が慶良間諸島に上陸して始まった。空襲や艦砲射撃など「鉄の暴風」と呼ばれる猛攻撃を加えた。激しい地上戦などで、日米双方で計20万人超が死亡し、うち一般住民は推計約9万4千人を占める。(同盟通信)

A boy working in a munitions factory, Okinawa, 1945. The Battle of Okinawa began on March 26, 1945 when US troops landed on the Kerama Islands. The intense offensive was called the "Tyhoon of Steel" consisting of air raids and naval gunfire. The brutal land battle that followed resulted in more than 200,000 deaths, including approximately 94,000 civilian residents. (Domei News Agency)

B29爆撃機による大阪空襲
B-29s bomb Osaka

1945(昭和20)年6月1日、第2回大阪大空襲で、工業地帯を爆撃する米軍のB29爆撃機。右側中央は大阪城の堀。大阪府内では44年12月〜45年8月14日に約50回の空襲があり、約1万5千人が犠牲になったとされる。米陸軍航空隊撮影。(ACME)

American B-29 bombers attacked industrial zones during the second great air raid of Osaka, June 1, 1945. At the right center is the moat of Osaka Castle. Around 50 air raids were conducted in Osaka Prefecture between December 1944 and August 14, 1945, killing some 15,000 people. Photo: US Army Air Corps. (ACME)

広島原爆のきのこ雲
Mushroom cloud over Hiroshima

1945（昭和20）年8月6日、広島への原爆投下約1時間後、米軍観測機が瀬戸内海上空から撮影したきのこ雲。原爆による熱線や爆風で街の広範囲が瞬時に壊滅、45年末までに約14万人が亡くなった。爆発時の初期放射線に加え、放射性物質を含む「黒い雨」などを浴びた人たちには白血病や各種がんが多発。今も健康被害や心の傷に苦しむ人は多い。

A US military observation aircraft flying over the Inland Sea captured the mushroom cloud roughly one hour after the atomic bomb was dropped on Hiroshima, August 6, 1945. The intense heat and blast of the A-bomb instantly destroyed a wide area of the city, and by the end of 1945, it had caused approximately 140,000 deaths. As a result of exposure to the initial radiation blast as well as the "black rain" containing radioactive fallout that followed, leukemia and various other types of cancer became very common. Thousands continue to suffer psychological and mental health impacts to this day.

グアムの収容所で玉音放送
Prisoners listen to Imperial broadcast at Guam camp

1945(昭和20)年8月15日、かつて日本軍が占領し、米軍が奪還したグアム島の捕虜収容所で、昭和天皇の「玉音放送」を整列して聞く日本軍捕虜。同放送は海外の戦地にいる日本軍将兵に向けても、遠距離地域にも電波が届く短波で放送された。(米軍撮影)

On August 15, 1945, Japanese prisoners of war lined up to listen to the declaration of surrender by Emperor Hirohito at a prison camp in Guam, an island retaken by the US military from Japan, which occupied the island during the war. The declaration was broadcast on shortwave radio in order to reach Japanese troops in distant foreign fields. (US Army photograph)

コラム

戦争とメディア

　メディアにとって戦争は最大のテーマであり、戦争を遂行する側にとってもメディア対策は戦局を有利に運ぶためにも決定的な課題だ。

　戦時中、新聞、ラジオを中心としたメディアは「大本営発表」に象徴される戦果の過大報道と事実のねじ曲げ、敵国への憎悪あおり立てなどを通じて戦争協力の役割を引き受けた。ナショナリズムへの迎合と、戦争が「売れる」コンテンツであるとの事情は、冷静・正確という報道の基本を往々にして忘れさせる。

　"国策通信社"として絶大な影響力を持った同盟通信は敗戦により連合国軍最高司令部（GHQ）による責任追及を覚悟して古野伊之助社長が自主的に解散を宣言、新たに共同通信、時事通信の分割発足を打ち出した。しかし戦時中の報道姿勢や内容を反省する認識は薄く、その後の検証作業も不十分だった。

　ベトナム戦争（1964〜75年）は国家権力がメディア支配に失敗し、米国を敗北に導いた最大要因ともされた。共産主義から自由社会を守るとしたものの民族自決を圧殺する大義なき戦争だったのに加えて、戦場での生々しいルポや写真、映像が伝えられることによって国民の疑念と反戦意識は爆発的に高まった。

　米政府は湾岸戦争（90〜91年）では徹底したメディア規制に乗り出した。従軍報道の便宜を図る一方、自由な報道は抑え込んだ。ベトナム戦争での批判に懲り、隣国を理不尽に侵略、征服しようとするイラクのフセイン政権を「悪者」として刷り込んで国際的合意による「正義の戦争」との宣伝に力を注いで一定の効果を上げた。これに続くイラク戦争（2003〜11年）も同様の情報戦略が取られたが、戦争の大義だった大量破壊兵器が見つからなかったことから大きな問題となり、便乗したメディアの側も深刻な反省を迫られた。

　情報技術が発達した現代の戦争はゲーム感覚で戦われる側面があり、戦場の実像や残虐性が伝わりにくくなっている。当事者はそれぞれ都合のいい情報を流し、何が真実か判然としない。デジタル化、SNSの普及はフェイクを生み出す温床ともなった。一方で、大きな組織的後ろ盾のないフリージャーナリストらによる果敢なリポートが存在感を発揮する事例も目立つ。

War and the Media

Column

War is a major theme for the media and an important tool for those waging it. Managing the media is a crucial task to shape public perception and secure an advantage in the conflict.

During wartime, media outlets like newspapers and radio often exaggerated military success, distorted facts, and incited hatred toward enemies, prioritizing nationalism and the profitability of war coverage over balanced and accurate reporting.

Domei News, Japan's government-controlled agency, dissolved after Japan's defeat, with Kyodo and Jiji Press taking its place. However, there was little reflection on the wartime reporting stance or its content, and subsequent efforts to scrutinize it were insufficient.

The Vietnam War (1964-75) marked a failure of the U.S. government's media control, which became a major factor in its defeat. Despite claiming to protect freedom from communism, the war was seen as unjust. Graphic reports, photos, and footage from the battlefield sparked widespread public doubt and anti-war sentiment.

In the Gulf War (1990-91), the U.S. government implemented strict media regulations by facilitating embedded reporting and suppressing independent journalism. Having learned from Vietnam, the U.S. presented Saddam Hussein's regime as the "villain," successfully promoting the war as a "just war" under international consensus. In the Iraq War (2003-11), a similar information strategy was used, but the failure to find weapons of mass destruction caused a major backlash. The media's complicity in this narrative led to significant reflection and critique.

Modern warfare, influenced by digital technology, makes it harder to convey the brutal reality of war. The spread of fake news has been exacerbated by social media, although independent journalists without major organizational backing have gained prominence for their courageous reporting.

同盟通信社長が社員を集め解散を説明
The President of Domei News Agency explains dissolution
1945（昭和20）年10月15日、東京・日比谷の同盟通信本社編集局に社員を集め、同月31日での同社解散を説明する古野伊之助社長（左奥）。古野は12月、A級戦争犯罪人容疑者として巣鴨刑務所に収容された。翌年8月、不起訴となり出所したが公職追放になった。（同盟通信）
October 15, 1945 – At the headquarters of Domei News Agency in Hibiya, Tokyo, President Inosuke Furuno (at left rear) informed employees of the decision to break up the agency. In December, Furuno was detained at Sugamo Prison as a suspected class A war criminal. The case was thrown out, and Furuno was released in August 1946, but he was expelled from the civil service. (Domei News Agency)

戦争で犠牲になったとされる日本人の数

広島原爆※ 約14万人
東京大空襲 約10万人
長崎原爆※ 約7万4000人
沖縄戦 約18万8000人

全体 約310万人
軍人ら 約230万人
市民ら 約80万人

※…広島と長崎は、1945年12月末までの数

長崎に投下された原爆のきのこ雲

東京大空襲で一面の焼け野原となった場所で生活する人たち

満州事変から太平洋戦争 主な戦場

- 1931年9月 柳条湖事件
- 37年7月 盧溝橋事件
- 45年8月 ソ連参戦
- 43年5月 アッツ島守備隊玉砕
- 44年7月 インパール作戦失敗
- 37年12月 南京占領
- 45年8月 広島、長崎に原爆投下
- 41年12月 香港占領
- 45年3月 硫黄島陥落
- 45年6月 沖縄守備隊全滅
- 44年7月 サイパン島陥落
- 42年6月 ミッドウェー海戦
- 42年1月 マニラ占領
- 41年12月 グアム島占領
- 41年12月 真珠湾攻撃
- 41年12月 英領マレー上陸
- 44年10月 レイテ沖海戦
- 43年2月 ガダルカナル島撤退
- 42年2月 シンガポール攻略
- 42年3月 ジャワ島上陸

⊗…日本の攻勢
✕…日本の敗退、被害

太平洋戦争で日本側の死者は約310万人だが、日本の侵略によって犠牲になったのはアジアだけで約2000万人とされている。

第2章：「平和国家」の虚実

　　　敗戦後の日本は社会の混乱、飢餓、精神の空虚に見舞われた。同時に少なくとも表面上の平和と民主主義がもたらされ、自由と希望、新しい文化の空気が広がった。
　世界的に見れば、第2次大戦のおびただしい犠牲と破壊の末に訪れたのは真の平和ではなく新たな戦争の火種と「冷戦」という名の新たな対立構造だった。日本はその中で「自由主義陣営」に属し、安全保障を米国に全面的に依存する国家になった。
　サンフランシスコ平和条約と独立の達成（1952年）、それと同時の日米安保条約締結、同条約改定（60年）、自動延長（70年）で米国の核の傘の下に安全が確保された形になった。米国は日本の防衛義務を負い、日本は基地を提供し駐留経費も「思いやり予算」として負担するという"双務性"があるとされている。
　その結果、直接の脅威からは免れて「経済立国」に専念する余地が生まれた。しかも朝鮮戦争（50〜53年）、ベトナム戦争（64〜75年）といった米国のアジアでの戦争の後背地として特需を得る"幸運"にも恵まれた。
　世界各地で地域紛争が激化しても日本は経済的影響だけを心配していればよかった。例えば第4次中東戦争（73年）時のアラブ産油国による「石油戦略」では、政府は資源確保、物価高騰への対策に追われ、トイレットペーパーを求めて庶民がスーパーに押し寄せるなどという社会的珍現象が生まれた。しかし、国際紛争解決に日本がどう貢献するかという機運は盛り上がらなかった。
　その一方で過去の戦争の反省や検証は深まっていない。米国の世界戦略に組み込まれる中で経済大国の道を突っ走り、国の在り方、安全保障や世界平和への貢献といった課題と真剣に向き合うことを怠った。
　米国はベトナム戦争の泥沼化の中で国力を衰退させ、日本との関係もドルショック（71年）、日米貿易摩擦の激化（80年代）など主に経済面でぎくしゃくすることになった。
　米国の国力低下とともに、いわゆる「安保ただ乗り」など厳しい視線が投げかけられるようになり、日本はそれまで後回しにしていた自国の安全への責任と軍事を含む国際貢献をどうするかの回答を迫られることになった。
　折から日本は昭和の終焉（89年）、バブルの崩壊（90年代初頭）と戦後の大きな曲がり角を迎えていた。

Chapter 2 : The Illusions of a "Peaceful Nation"

Postwar Japan faced chaos, hunger, and spiritual emptiness. At the same time, at least on the surface, peace and democracy were introduced, spreading an atmosphere of freedom, hope, and new culture.

Globally, what followed the immense sacrifices and destruction of World War II was not genuine peace but new seeds of conflict and a new structure of confrontation called the "Cold War." Within this context, Japan became part of the "liberal camp" and a nation that fully depended on the United States for its security.

With the signing of the San Francisco Peace Treaty and the achievement of independence in 1952, the simultaneous signing of the Japan-U.S. Security Treaty, its revision in 1960, and its automatic extension in 1970, Japan's safety was secured under the U.S. nuclear umbrella. While the United States was said to bear the obligation of defending Japan, Japan provided bases and covered the costs of stationing troops through the "sympathy budget," maintaining a semblance of mutual responsibility.

As a result, Japan was freed from direct threats, creating room to focus on becoming an "economic nation." Furthermore, Japan was fortunate enough to benefit from special procurements as a rear base for U.S. wars in Asia, such as the Korean War (1950-53) and the Vietnam War (1964-75).

Even as regional conflicts intensified across the world, Japan only needed to worry about economic impacts. For example, during the Fourth Middle East War (1973), the "oil strategy" of Arab oil-producing countries forced the government to secure resources and address rising prices, resulting in unusual social phenomena such as citizens rushing to supermarkets in search of toilet paper. However, there was no surge of momentum for Japan to consider how it could contribute to resolving international conflicts.

On the other hand, reflection on past wars and examination of Japan's path to modernization did not deepen. While being incorporated into the United States' global strategy, Japan single-mindedly pursued the path of becoming an economic power, neglecting to seriously address issues such as the country's identity, security, and contributions to world peace.

Amid the quagmire of the Vietnam War, the United States experienced a decline in national strength, which strained Japan-U.S. relations, particularly in economic terms, as seen with the Nixon Shock (1971) and escalating trade frictions in the 1980s.

As U.S. power waned, harsh criticism began to arise, such as accusations of Japan "free-riding" on security arrangements. Japan was then forced to confront questions about its responsibility for its own security and its role in international contributions, including military involvement, which it had postponed until that point.

At the same time, Japan reached a significant turning point in its postwar history, marked by the end of the Showa era (1989) and the collapse of the bubble economy in the early 1990s.

マッカーサー司令官が厚木に到着
General MacArthur lands in Atsugi

1945（昭和20）年8月30日、C54輸送機「バターン号」で神奈川県の厚木飛行場に到着、コーンパイプを手にタラップを下りるダグラス・マッカーサー連合国軍最高司令官。当時65歳。マッカーサーは日本で新憲法制定や財閥解体、農地改革などに取り組んだ。（同盟通信）

On August 30, 1945, General Douglas MacArthur arrived at Atsugi Air Base in Kanagawa Prefecture aboard the C-54 transport aircraft "Bataan." He was 65 then and was seen climbing down the gangway with a pipe in hand. MacArthur undertook the establishment of the new Japanese constitution, the dissolution of the zaibatsu conglomerates, and the implementation of land reform. (Domei News Agency)

米戦艦ミズーリで降伏文書調印式
Signing of surrender document aboard the USS Missouri

1945(昭和20)年9月2日、東京湾に停泊した米戦艦ミズーリで日本の降伏文書調印式が行われ、太平洋戦争が終結した。艦橋に群がる乗組員と報道陣が見守る中、日本側(甲板中央)は全権代表の重光葵外相、梅津美治郎参謀総長が、連合国側はマッカーサー最高司令官ら米、英、ソ連など9カ国代表が署名した。(米国防総省提供)

The Pacific War officially ended by the signing of the document of Japan's surrender aboard the warship USS Missouri in Tokyo Bay, September 2, 1945. As the crew and press watch on from the bridge, the document was signed by delegates Foreign Minister Mamoru Shigemitsu and Chief of the Army General Staff Yoshijiro Umezu on the Japanese side (center of the deck), and General MacArthur and the representatives of eight other Allied nations. (Photo: US Department of Defense)

被爆1カ月後の長崎
Nagasaki one month after the atomic bombing

1945（昭和20）年9月、原爆投下から約1カ月後の長崎で、被災者が自宅のあった場所に建てた掘っ立て小屋。被爆地に初めて入った米報道陣が撮影した。長崎では同年末までに死者は約7万4千人、重軽傷者は約7万5千人に上ったと推計されている。（ACME）

A hut built by a survivor on the site of their former home, approximately a month after the dropping of the atomic bomb on Nagasaki, September 1945. The photo was taken by the first US press group to enter the bomb zone. It is estimated that by the end of 1945, the A-bomb had killed some 74,000 people in Nagasaki and injured 75,000 others. (ACME)

青空教室で元気に授業
Lively outdoor lesson

1945（昭和20）年9月25日、屋外の青空教室で元気に授業を受ける児童たち。戦争中の空襲で国民学校の校舎は焼け落ちてしまったが、子どもたちの表情には明るさも。雨の日は自宅学習だった。（同盟通信）

Schoolchildren enjoyed a lesson in an open-air classroom on September 25, 1945. Despite the destruction of their school buildings by air raids during the war, these children wore somewhat bright expressions. On rainy days, children would learn at home. (Domei News Agency)

バラック住宅前で布団干し
Futon drying out the front of the slum dwellings

1945（昭和20）年10月12日、都内の空襲による焼け跡で、久しぶりの晴天に布団などを干すバラック住宅に住む女性。空襲で家を失った人たちは、焼け残りのトタンなどで造ったバラックの家での生活を余儀なくされた。電気や水道などが無い不自由な生活で、物資や食料の不足が深刻だった。（同盟通信）

Women residing in a "barrack" hut amid the destruction of incendiary air raids in Tokyo take the opportunity of a rare fine day to dry their futon mattresses, October 12, 1945. Those whose homes were destroyed in the air raids were forced to live in makeshift dwellings made of galvanized iron and other materials remaining intact after the firebombing. Without electricity or running water, life was difficult, and there was a severe shortage of materials and food. (Domei News Agency)

進駐軍兵士でにぎわうキャバレー
Occupation troops enjoying the cabaret

1945（昭和20）年11月、進駐軍兵士らでにぎわう東京・銀座のキャバレー。連合国軍の到着に先立ち「特殊慰安施設協会（RAA）」が設立され、進駐軍兵士向け慰安施設の開業を進めた。女性たちは街頭広告や新聞広告などを通じて集められた。

Occupation soldiers enjoyed the cabaret in Ginza, Tokyo, November 1945. Ahead of the arrival of Allied troops, the Recreation and Amusement Association (RAA) was set up and brothels established to service them. Women were recruited by posters put up on streets and newspaper advertisement.

新橋駅前の闇市
Black market at Shimbashi Station

1946（昭和21）年2月5日、終戦から約半年、食料や衣料などを求め東京・新橋駅前の闇市を埋めた大勢の人たち。終戦直後の新橋駅周辺には日本最大規模の闇市が広がり、バラックの飲食店が密集した。闇市には悪質な露天商がはびこり、犯罪の温床でもあった。

Around six months after the end of the war, the black market in front of Shimbashi Station, Tokyo, is thronged with people seeking food, clothing, and other supplies on February 5, 1946. In the immediate postwar period, the area around Shimbashi Station was the biggest black market in Japan. There were also a lot of stall-like restaurants in the neighborhood. The black market was plagued by underhanded dealings and a hotbed of criminality.

広島原爆から1年
A year on from the bomb in Hiroshima

1946（昭和21）年8月5日、原爆投下から1年、市内のデパート屋上から撮影した広島市街。若いカップルが見つめる先には焼け野原が広がる。1発の原爆で市街地は壊滅、復興の兆しはまだ見えていない。

The city of Hiroshima as seen from the roof of a department store one year after the dropping of the atomic bomb, August 5, 1946. A young couple gazes across a desolate landscape. A cityscape laid waste by a single blast, with no signs of recovery yet evident.

日本国憲法が成立
Establishment of the Japanese constitution

1946(昭和21)年10月7日、戦後日本の出発点となる日本国憲法が衆院で可決、成立した。連合国軍総司令部(GHQ)の草案を基に政府が大日本帝国憲法改正案を作り、帝国議会が修正した。軍部の暴走を許した大日本帝国憲法を全面改正し、国民主権、基本的人権の尊重、平和主義の3原則を定めた。11月3日に公布され、翌47年5月3日に施行された。

The new Japanese constitution, the starting point of postwar Japan, is approved by the Diet and established, October 7, 1946. Based on a draft from the General Headquarters (GHQ), the Japanese government created a proposal for amendment of the Imperial constitution, which was then revised by the Imperial Diet. The Imperial constitution, which had allowed free reign to the military, was completely overhauled to incorporate the three principles of popular sovereignty, respect for fundamental human rights, and pacifism. Promulgated on November 3, the new constitution became effective on May 3, 1947.

満州からの引き揚げ孤児
Orphans from Manchuria

1946（昭和21）年12月5日、東京・品川駅に到着した満州（現中国東北部）からの引き揚げ孤児たち。両親の遺骨を抱く少女など、幼くして両親を亡くした子どもたちは上野の施設に入り、縁故先などに引き取られるのを待った。厚生労働省によると、戦後各地からの軍人・軍属と民間人を合わせた引き揚げ者の総数は約630万人。

Orphans arriving from Manchuria (present-day northeast China) at Shinagawa Station, Tokyo, December 5, 1946. The young children, one of whom is a girl clutching the remains of her parents, entered an orphanage in Ueno to await adoption by their relatives or new families. According to the Ministry of Health, Labour and Welfare, the total number of Japanese repatriated from warzones around the world, including the military, their families, and civilians, totaled around 6.3 million.

シベリア抑留者が舞鶴に帰国
Siberian detainees return home at Maizuru

1946（昭和21）年12月8日、シベリアからの復員兵ら2555人を乗せた帰還第1船「大久丸」が京都・舞鶴港に入港。極寒の地で収容所生活を送った人たちが上陸を待つ。終戦後、ソ連軍は満州や朝鮮半島で日本兵や民間人の身柄を拘束し、シベリア地域などで強制労働を課した。厚生労働省は、シベリア抑留者は約57万5千人で約5万5千人が死亡したとしている。

The first ship repatriating 2,555 former soldiers from Siberia, the Daikyu-maru, enters the port of Maizuru, Kyoto Prefecture, December 8, 1946. For these men who survived imprisonment in the extreme cold of Siberia, landing could not come soon enough. After the war, the Red Army rounded up Japanese soldiers and civilians from Manchuria and the Korean Peninsula and pressed them into forced labor in Siberia and other regions of the Soviet Union. Of some 575,000 detainees in Siberia, around 55,000 did not survive.

法廷の東条元首相
Former Prime Minister Hideki Tojo on trial

1947（昭和22）年12月29日、連合国が日本の指導者の戦争責任を裁いた極東国際軍事裁判（東京裁判）の法廷で、上を向いて弁護人による書面の朗読を聞く被告の東条英機元首相。48年11月、A級戦犯として起訴された28人のうち、途中で死亡するなどした3人を除く25人全員が有罪となり、東条ら7人が絞首刑となった。

On December 29, 1947, at the trial of the International Military Tribunal for the Far East to judge the responsibility for war crimes by the Japanese leadership (Tokyo Trial), defendant Hideki Tojo listened with face upturned to his oral statement being read out by his lawyer. In November 1948, of the 28 defendants accused of being Class A war criminals, apart from the three partway through the trial, all 25 were found guilty. Former Prime Minister Tojo and six others were executed by hanging.

米独立記念日を祝い有楽町を行進
American Independence Day parade in Yurakucho

1948（昭和23）年7月5日、米独立記念日（7月4日）を祝い東京・有楽町を行進する進駐軍部隊。米軍、英連邦軍部隊など数千人の将兵が皇居前広場でマッカーサー連合国軍最高司令官の閲兵を受けた。丸の内から日比谷のパレードの沿道では約20万人が見物。

Occupied troops held a parade to celebrate US Independence Day (July 4th) in Yurakucho, Tokyo, on July 5, 1948. Several thousand US and Commonwealth troops were inspected by General MacArthur at the plaza in front of the Imperial Palace. Some 200,000 spectators lined the road between Marunouchi and Hibiya.

上野で路上生活者の一斉保護
Mass removal of homeless, Ueno

1949（昭和24）年12月6日、東京・上野駅地下道を中心に、都民生局（当時）や上野警察署が百数十人態勢で大がかりな路上生活者の一斉保護を行った。約千人が都内の保護施設、病院、母子寮などに収容された。

In the area around the underground passages of Ueno Station, Tokyo, the (former) Metropolitan Hygiene Department and the Ueno Police Station conducted a mass removal of homeless people from the streets on December 6, 1949. Roughly a thousand people were taken to facilities, hospitals, and homes for mothers and children across Tokyo.

在日米軍基地で空襲に備え対空砲
Anti-aircraft gun on the US Army Japan base

1950(昭和25)年、日本の米軍基地で空襲に備える対空砲と、朝鮮半島に出撃するF80戦闘機。朝鮮戦争はこの年の6月25日、北朝鮮が韓国に攻め込んで勃発、米国とソ連の対立を背景に、国際紛争に発展した。太平洋戦争後に米軍が接収した日本各地の基地からは戦闘機や爆撃機が出撃、航空輸送にも中核的な機能を果たした。(50年7月1日米軍提供)

Anti-aircraft guns were prepared for air raids and F-80 Shooting Star aircrafts were readied for flying sorties to the Korean Peninsula on a US base in Japan, 1950. It was the year of the outbreak of the Korean War when North Korean forces invaded the South on June 25, developing into an international conflict amid the standoff between the US and the USSR. The bases across Japan acquired by the US military after World War II played a core role in launching sorties of fighter planes and bombers, as well as air transportation. (US Army, July 1, 1950)

整列する警察予備隊の隊員
National Police Reservists line up

1950(昭和25)年8月25日、東京都北多摩郡小平町(現小平市)の東京管区警察学校のグラウンドで整列する警察予備隊の隊員。6月に勃発した朝鮮戦争に在日米軍が出兵、日本の治安維持のため7月8日、マッカーサー連合国軍最高司令官は日本政府に7万5千人の警察予備隊の創設を指示した。52年保安隊、54年自衛隊に改組された。

Members of the National Police Reserve line up on the field of the Kanto District National Police Academy in Kodaira town, Kitatama District, Tokyo Metropolis (present-day Kodaira City), August 25, 1950. On July 8, the Supreme Commander for the Allied Powers, General MacArthur, instructed the Japanese government to establish a 75,000-man police reserve force to maintain security in Japan due to the outbreak of the Korean War in June and the dispatch of US troops stationed in Japan to the Korean Peninsula. In 1952, it was renamed the National Safety Force, and in 1954, it was reorganized as the Japan Self-Defense Forces.

神戸港で朝鮮戦争の装備や物資を船積み
Ship being loaded with equipment and supplies for the Korean War, Kobe Port

1950（昭和25）年9月、朝鮮戦争の仁川上陸作戦のため、神戸港で装備と補給物資を船積みする米第1海兵師団兵士。当時日本は連合国の占領下にあったが、「朝鮮特需」と呼ばれた米軍の戦時関連物資の需要急増により好景気がもたらされ、敗戦から復興を遂げるきっかけになった。（米国防総省提供）

Troops of the US 1st Marine Division loaded equipment and fresh supplies onto a ship at Kobe Port for the Incheon landing during the Korean War in September 1950. At the time, Japan was under Allied Occupation, but with the "extra demand from Korea", the increased demand for war-related goods for the US military led to an economic boom and triggered the recovery from war defeat. (Photo: US Department of Defense)

朝鮮戦争で避難する人たち
Refugees from the Korean War

1951(昭和26)年1月、荷物を持ちソウルから南に脱出する避難民の長い列。朝鮮戦争は50年に勃発。53年に板門店で国連軍、中国人民義勇軍、朝鮮人民軍の各代表が休戦協定に署名した。協定により、北緯38度線付近の軍事境界線で韓国と北朝鮮の南北に分断された。(米陸軍撮影)

A long line of refugees fleeing south from Seoul with their belongings, January 1951. The Korean War broke out in 1950. The Korean Armistice Agreement was signed in 1953 at Panmunjom by representatives of the United Nations Command, China's People's Volunteer Army, and the Korean Army. The armistice created a demilitarized zone (DMZ) near the 38th parallel north, which divided the peninsula between North Korea and South Korea. (Photo: US Army)

対日平和条約調印を祝い日の丸
Hinomaru was raised to celebrate the signing of the San Francisco Peace Treaty

1951（昭和26）年9月9日、対日平和条約調印を祝い日の丸が掲げられた東京・銀座。8日（日本時間9日午前）に米サンフランシスコで、日本と連合国の戦争状態を終結させるサンフランシスコ平和条約が調印された。

The Hinomaru Japanese flag was raised over Ginza, Tokyo, in celebration of the signing of the Treaty of Peace with Japan, September 9, 1951. The signing of the peace treaty in San Francisco on September 8 (the morning of September 9, Japan time) ended the legal state of war between Japan and the Allied Powers.

保安隊戦車が狭い道路を行進
National Safety Force tanks march on a narrow road

1953（昭和28）年1月22日、警察予備隊を改組して前年10月に発足した保安隊のM24戦車16両が群馬、埼玉両県を初行進した。行程69㌔の長距離訓練で、商店や民家が連なる狭い道路を行進する戦車隊のごう音と砂ぼこりが住民を驚かせた。M24は米軍から供与された。54年7月、保安隊を陸上自衛隊、領海警備を担う警備隊を海上自衛隊に改組し、航空自衛隊を新設して陸海空の3隊がそろった。

Sixteen Light Tank M24s of the National Safety Force, established in October 1952 from the reorganization of the National Police Reserve, were on the road for the first time in Gunma and Saitama prefectures, January 22, 1953. As a long-distance training exercise, the 69km route included narrow roads lined by shops and civilian homes, and the dust and noise of the tanks surprised local residents. The M24 tanks were provided by the US military. In July 1954, the National Safety Force was reorganized into the Ground Self-Defense Force. Additionally, a guard force responsible for protecting territorial waters was established as the Maritime Self-Defense Force. At the same time, the Air Self-Defense Force was newly established, completing the formation of the three branches of Self-Defense Forces.

傷痍軍人が募金を呼びかけ
Soliciting donations for wounded veterans

1953(昭和28)年12月27日、大勢の人たちが行き交う歳末の大阪で、白い服で募金を呼びかける傷痍軍人。日中戦争や太平洋戦争で負傷したり病気になったりした元軍人らで組織する「日本傷痍軍人会」は、多い時には35万人の会員がいたが、2013年時点で約5千人にまで減少。高齢化も進んで組織の存続が難しくなったとして同年に解散した。

On the busy streets of Osaka before the New Year, wounded former soldiers dressed in a white kimono asked for donations on December 27, 1953. The Japanese Disabled Veterans Association, made up of former soldiers injured or taken ill during the Sino-Japanese War and the Pacific War, boasted a membership of 350,000 at its peak but as of 2013, had shrunk to around 5,000 members. The Association disbanded that year due to aging and organizational unsustainability.

ビキニ環礁で米国の水爆実験
US tests hydrogen bomb at Bikini Atoll

1954(昭和29)年3月、太平洋・マーシャル諸島北部のビキニ環礁で実施された米国の水爆実験。米軍は46〜58年、ビキニ環礁とエニウェトク環礁で計67回の核実験を行った。3月1日に実験された水爆「ブラボー」は広島に投下された原爆の約千倍の威力があり、周辺島民や周辺を航行していた静岡県焼津市のマグロ漁船「第五福竜丸」などの乗組員らが放射性降下物「死の灰」を浴びて被ばく、9月に無線長、久保山愛吉さんが亡くなった。原水爆禁止運動が広がる契機になった。(米エネルギー省提供)

The US conducted a hydrogen bomb test on Bikini Atoll in the Pacific's northern Marshall Islands in March 1954. Between 1946 and 1958, the US military conducted 67 nuclear tests at Bikini Atoll and Enewetak Atoll. The Castle Bravo hydrogen bomb test of March 1 was around a thousand times more powerful than the bomb dropped on Hiroshima. Radioactive fallout (black rain) from the test fell on islanders living on nearby islands as well as the crew of the Daigo Fukuryu Maru (Lucky Dragon No. 5), a tuna fishing boat originating from Yaizu, Shizuoka that was passing through the area. The boat's chief radio operator, Aikichi Kuboyama, died of radiation poisoning in September, giving fresh impetus to the movement to ban atomic and hydrogen bomb tests. (Photo: US Department of Energy)

ビキニで被ばくのマグロを検査
Testing of tuna irradiated at Bikini

1954(昭和29)年3月16日、東京・築地の中央卸売市場で、ビキニ環礁で被ばくした「第五福竜丸」のマグロを測定器で調べる科学研究所員と東京都衛生局員。測定の結果、水揚げのマグロから放射線が検出された。政府は周辺海域で操業または通過した船の放射線検査を実施。東京や高知などの18港で同年12月までに延べ856隻が、約486㌧の汚染魚を廃棄した。

At Tsukiji Central Wholesale Market, Tokyo on March 16, 1954, scientists and Tokyo Metropolitan Government Bureau of Public Health officials tested tuna from the Daigo Fukuryu Maru, which was exposed to radiation at Bikini Atoll. Results revealed that the tuna was contaminated. The government conducted radiation testing of all boats that had fished or passed through the surrounding seas. By December 1954, some 486 tons of contaminated fish were disposed of from 856 vessels landing at 18 ports, including Tokyo and Kochi.

披露された自衛隊旗と自衛艦旗
Flags of the ground and maritime SDF unveiled

1954（昭和29）年6月26日、東京・越中島の保安庁で、7月1日の防衛庁と陸海空3自衛隊の発足を前に披露された自衛隊旗（左）と自衛艦旗。手前は木村篤太郎保安庁長官（左）が書き上げた「防衛庁」と「防衛大学校」の看板。自衛隊は2024年7月1日、発足から70年を迎えた。

The flags of the SDF(Self-Defence Forces) ground forces (left) and maritime forces were unveiled on June 26, 1954, at the National Safety Agency, Etchujima, Tokyo, ahead of the establishment of the Defense Agency and the three branches of the SDF on July 1. The calligraphy signs in front for "Defense Agency" and "Defense Academy" were written by National Safety Agency Commissioner Tokutaro Kimura (left). The SDF marked its 70th anniversary on July 1, 2024.

日米新安保条約を強行採決
Forced passage of US-Japan Security Treaty

1960（昭和35）年5月19日、衆院本会議場で与野党議員にもまれながらマイクをにぎり会期延長を諮る清瀬一郎議長。日米新安全保障条約をめぐる混乱から清瀬議長は警官500人を院内に導入。20日午前0時過ぎ、新安保条約を自民党単独で強行採決した。新安保条約は在日米軍への基地提供が中心だった旧安保条約を改定、米軍に日本防衛を義務付けた。

Surrounded by opposition Diet members, Speaker of the House of Representatives Ichiro Kiyose gripped the microphone and called a vote on extending the Diet session, May 19, 1960. Speaker Kiyose called 500 police officers into the Diet amid the uproar over the US-Japan Security Treaty. After midnight on May 20, the Liberal Democratic Party alone forced the passage of the revised Security Treaty. While the previous Security Treaty was principally concerned with allowing US forces to be stationed in Japan, the revision mandated the US to defend Japan if attacked by a third party.

米軍立川基地めぐり砂川闘争
The Sunagawa Struggle over the Tachikawa Air Base

1955（昭和30）年9月13日、東京都砂川町（現立川市）で米軍立川基地拡張のための強制測量が始まり、反対派と警官が激しく衝突。反対運動の激化で流血事件が繰り返され、米軍は福生市などに位置する横田基地に移駐した。77年に立川基地は返還され、昭和記念公園や陸上自衛隊駐屯地、立川広域防災基地などになった。

Activists opposing the compulsory survey undertaken to extend the runway of the US Air Force Tachikawa base clashed fiercely with police officers in Sunagawa Town, Tokyo (present-day Tachikawa City), September 13, 1955. After recurring bloody clashes with an increasingly radical opposition movement, the US military relocated to Yokota Air Base in Fussa City. In 1977, the Tachikawa base was returned to Japan and developed as Showa Memorial Park, a ground SDF garrison and a Tachikawa Wide-area Disaster Management Base.

国会議事堂前のデモ隊
Demonstration outside the National Diet Building

1960(昭和35)年6月18日、学生や労働者のデモ隊に包囲された国会議事堂。安保改定で「日本が戦争に巻き込まれる」という懸念が強まり反対運動に発展、新安保条約の自然承認前日のこの日、頂点に達した。国会周辺を含めデモ参加者は主催者発表で約33万人。全国各地でもデモが行われ、革新勢力のほか学者や文化人も参加した。23日には条約の批准書が交換され発効、岸信介首相は安保をめぐる混乱の責任を取る形で退陣した。

The National Diet Building was surrounded by protesting students and workers on June 18, 1960. The movement opposing the revision of the US-Japan Security Treaty was driven by concern that Japan would be caught up in other countries' wars, and it reached its zenith the day before the revised Security Treaty was to automatically take effect. Organizers estimated the number of protesters outside the Diet at 330,000. Demonstrations took place simultaneously around Japan, with the progressive forces joined by scholars and people of culture. The Security Treaty entered into force with the exchange of letters of ratification on June 23. Prime Minister Nobusuke Kishi resigned to take responsibility for the upheaval caused by the Security Treaty revision.

空爆から帰投した米攻撃機
US attack aircraft return from raids

1965（昭和40）年8月27日、南ベトナム解放民族戦線基地の爆撃を終えサイゴン（現ホーチミン市）から約240㌔の南シナ海に展開する米空母コーラルシーに着艦するA1H攻撃機。南北に分断されていたベトナムで、南を支持していた米国は64年のトンキン湾事件を契機に65年から北ベトナムへの空爆を始め、本格的な戦争に突入した。

A-1H Skyraiders returned to the USS Coral Sea, stationed some 240km from Saigon (present-day Ho Chi Minh City) in the South China Sea after completing missions attacking bases of the Liberation Army of South Vietnam ("Viet Cong"), August 27, 1965. After the Gulf of Tonkin incident in 1964, the US engaged directly in the war supporting South Vietnam, starting air raids on North Vietnam in 1965.

新宿で燃料輸送列車炎上
Fire on fuel train, Shinjuku

1967（昭和42）年8月8日、東京・新宿駅構内で、米軍横田基地行きの航空機燃料を積んだ列車と貨物列車が衝突。漏れた燃料に引火し爆発、炎上した。電車約1100本が運休、約200万人の足が乱れた。ベトナム戦争用燃料の輸送実態が分かり、反戦運動を刺激した。

On August 8, 1967, a train carrying jet fuel bound for Yokota Air Base collided with another freight train inside Shinjuku Station. Spilt fuel combusted and exploded, causing the cancellation of approximately 1,100 train services and disrupting the plans of around 2 million passengers. The incident revealed the truth about fuel transportation during the Vietnam War, which stimulated the anti-war movement.

新宿駅地下広場でフォークゲリラ
The folk guerilla concert at the underground square of Shinjuku Station

1969（昭和44）年5月24日、東京・新宿駅西口地下広場で、ギターを抱えて歌う若者と地下広場を埋め尽くした人たち。ベ平連（ベトナムに平和を！市民連合）などの若者が中心となって反戦フォークソングを歌う集会で、「フォークゲリラ」と呼ばれた。一時は約8千人が集まったが、警察が「広場ではなく通路」として規制に乗り出し、混乱の末に消滅した。

The Shinjuku Station West Exit underground plaza crowded with young people singing and playing the guitars, May 24, 1969. Youth gathered to sing folk songs, including Beheiren (the Citizen's League for Peace in Vietnam), and were termed "folk guerillas." The gatherings attracted up to 8,000 people, but once the police declared that the plaza was, in fact, a thoroughfare and launched a crackdown, the gatherings dissipated after some upheaval.

過激派が新宿駅構内を占拠
Shinjuku Station occupied by radicals

1968(昭和43)年10月21日、ベトナム戦争に反対する「国際反戦デー」の夜、東京の新宿駅で、米軍のジェット燃料輸送を阻止しようとする過激派学生や群衆による暴動事件が発生した。数千人が駅周辺に集結、一部が駅構内に乱入し放火や投石で電車、信号機などを破壊。駅構内を占拠し暴徒化したとして16年ぶりに騒乱罪が適用され、700人以上が逮捕された。

On the evening of the "International Anti-War Day" opposing the Vietnam War, October 21, 1968, violence broke out as radical students and crowds attempted to prevent shipments of jet fuel by the US military at Shinjuku Station. Thousands gathered around the station, and then some of the crowd entered the station, setting fires and throwing stones, damaging trains and signals. In response to the occupation and violent acts, the Anti-Riot Law was invoked for the first time in 16 years, and over 700 arrests were made.

米軍嘉手納基地にB52爆撃機着陸
B-52s landed at Kadena Air Base

1968（昭和43）年12月11日、ドラッグシュート（制動傘）を開いて沖縄県の米軍嘉手納基地に着陸したB52戦略爆撃機。嘉手納は極東最大の米空軍基地。この年2月、ベトナム戦争の本格化に伴い、B52の嘉手納への常駐配備が始まった。11月には離陸に失敗したB52が墜落し、搭載していた爆弾が爆発炎上。付近の住民が負傷、民家に被害が出た。住民の反対運動が高まり、最終的にB52部隊は嘉手納から撤退した。

A B-52 bomber deployed its drag chute upon landing at Kadena Air Base, Okinawa, December 11, 1968. Kadena was the largest US Air Force base in the Far East. In February 1968, with the US fully engaged in the Vietnam War, B-52s were deployed to Kadena on a permanent basis. In November that year, a B-52 crashed on take-off and caught fire and its bomb load detonated. The resulting blast damaged nearby houses and injured residents. The local opposition movement grew and eventually, the B-52s were removed from Kadena.

本土復帰の日に抗議の県民総決起大会
Protestors gathered to oppose on the day of the reversion of Okinawa to Japan

1972(昭和47)年5月15日、この日沖縄県が本土に復帰した。東京と同時に政府主催の「沖縄復帰記念式典」が開催された那覇市民会館に隣接する与儀公園では「5・15県民総決起大会」が開かれた。復帰の祝賀ムードとは対照的に、基地の負担が軽減されないままの本土復帰に抗議する大会だった。52年4月発効のサンフランシスコ平和条約で日本は主権を回復したが、奄美群島は53年、小笠原諸島は68年、沖縄は72年まで、それぞれ米施政権下に置かれていた。

Okinawa was returned to Japan on May 15, 1972. Official government ceremonies to mark the occasion were held simultaneously in Tokyo and in Naha Civic Hall, while a protest meeting, "May 15th Okinawa Rally," was held in Yogi Park, which is adjacent to Naha Civic Hall. In contrast to the celebratory mood surrounding reversion, the protest meeting of Okinawans opposed reversion without accompanying reduction in the burden imposed by US bases. While the San Francisco Treaty had returned full sovereignty to Japan when it entered into effect in April 1952, the Amami Islands remained under US control until 1953, the Ogasawara Islands until 1968, and Okinawa until 1972.

ネオン輝く銀座
Neon Ginza

1973(昭和48)年4月25日、華やかなネオンが輝く東京・銀座。

Ginza, Tokyo was illuminated by bright neon lights, April 25, 1973.

ネオン消えた銀座
Neon lights go dark in Ginza

1974(昭和49)年1月16日、広告のネオンが消された東京・銀座。第4次中東戦争をきっかけに原油価格が急騰、消費国はパニックに陥った。政府は大口需要家の石油消費抑制、大口電力の使用規制、マイカーの使用自粛、デパートやスーパーの営業時間短縮、テレビ深夜放送の休止、広告塔の時間短縮など強力な行政指導を行った。銀座のネオンも消えることに。「狂乱物価」に見舞われた日本は74年度、戦後初めてマイナス成長に転落。高度経済成長が終わった。

Neon advertising was switched off in Ginza, Tokyo, January 16, 1974. Due to the Yom Kippur War in the Middle East, the price of oil spiked and oil-consuming countries descended into a state of panic. The Japanese government placed restrictions on consumption by large oil and electricity users, while strong administrative guidance was given to drivers to limit their vehicle use, to department stores and supermarkets to open with shorter hours, suspend late-night TV, and shorten the operating hours of advertising billboards. The neon lights of Ginza also went dark. Fiscal 1974 was the year that "prices went crazy," and Japan recorded its first economic recession since the war. It was the end of the high-growth era.

30年間潜伏生活の小野田さん救出
Onoda rescued after 30 years in hiding

1974（昭和49）年3月10日、フィリピン・ルバング島の空軍施設でランクード空軍司令官に軍刀を渡し挙手の礼をする元日本軍少尉、小野田寛郎さん（中央）。太平洋戦争後約30年間、同島のジャングルで潜伏生活を送り、探しにきた元上官らの説得を受け入れて山を降りた。自作の服、戦闘帽、脚半、運動靴姿だった。2年前の72年には米領グアムで元日本兵、横井庄一さんが救出された。

Hiroo Onoda (C), a lieutenant in the Imperial Japanese Army, hands over his military sword and saluted Major General Rancudo of the Philippine Air Force at a radar base in Lubang Island, Philippines, March 10, 1974. He was wearing clothes he made himself, a battle hat, Japanese gaiters, and sneakers. For 30 years since the end of the war, he lived as a guerilla in the jungle of the island and finally was convinced to come out of the mountains by his former commanding officers. Two years before, in 1972, another former Japanese soldier, Shoichi Yokoi, had been rescued from the US territory of Guam.

ベルリンの壁崩壊
Fall of the Berlin Wall

1989（平成元）年11月10日未明、東ドイツ政府の国境開放後、東側からベルリンの壁をよじ登る市民たち。ベルリンの壁は東西冷戦下の61年、東ドイツ当局が西ドイツの飛び地だった西ベルリンへの自国民の逃亡を防ぐため建設を始めた。西ベルリンの周囲155㌔に高さ約3・6㍍のコンクリート製の壁を築き、十数カ所の検問所を設置した。9日、民主化要求のうねりを背景に東ドイツ当局が検問所を開放した。（ロイター）

Citizens clambered up the Berlin Wall from the east side after the East German government opened the borders in the early hours of the morning of November 10, 1989. Construction of the Berlin Wall was begun by the East German authorities during the Cold War in 1961 to prevent its citizens from escaping to the West German enclave of West Berlin. The 155km-long concrete wall surrounding West Berlin was built to a height of 3.6m, with a dozen checkpoints installed along its length. On December 9, the groundswell in favor of democratization led the East German authorities to open the checkpoints. (Reuters)

コラム　　　　　　　　　　「未完の戦後処理」

　未曽有の被害をもたらした末に敗戦した日本に課せられた賠償責任と戦後処理は巨大かつ複雑なものになった。そしてそれは理想とは程遠く、不十分で、今なお完結していない。
　国家間レベルの戦後処理は、1951年のサンフランシスコ講和会議と翌年の平和条約の発効・独立回復で一区切りがついたとされる。第1次世界大戦後の過酷な賠償金がナチズムを生む一因となった反省や、冷戦構造の中での思惑などから米欧主要国からの巨額の賠償金要求は免れた。しかしソ連などとの講和は持ち越されて全面講和とはならず、アジア各国との賠償、国交問題もその後の個別交渉に委ねられた。
　領土をめぐってもソ連との間の北方領土をはじめとして今も解決に至らず、中国大陸、朝鮮半島などの侵略、植民地支配で被害は個人補償や民族感情なども含めて深刻な形で現在に尾を引いている。北朝鮮との間の賠償問題が残されていることも忘れてはならない。
　そのような対外的な戦後処理に加えて、日本国民が受けた被害に対する賠償はさらに複雑で困難な課題だった。
　終戦時海外には約660万人の邦人が在留しており、引き揚げには大きな苦難と犠牲を生んだ。外地で保有し、没収された財産は一切補償されなかった。ソ連軍によってシベリアなどに抑留された約60万人のうち約6万人が死亡したとされ、抑留者に対する補償問題は戦後長く置き去りにされた。
　戦争の記憶が薄れた1981年には旧満州（中国東北部）などに取り残され、養父母らに育てられた中国残留日本人孤児の肉親捜しのための訪日調査が始まり、あらためて傷跡の深さを人々に思い知らせた。南方の島々などに残された数知れない戦没者の遺骨収集も遅々として進んでいないのが実情だ。
　国内で空襲などの被害を受けた民間人への補償も未解決だ。国に雇用された形の軍人、軍属らに対する補償が行われているのと比べて不公平だとの指摘に対して国は「民間人は日本国民が等しく受けた被害として耐え忍ぶしかない」と、「受忍論」を基に補償を拒否し、度重なる司法判断でも退けられている。
　領土問題、侵略・植民地支配の清算、民間人に対する被害補償、どれを取っても解決が難しいのは間違いない。しかしすべて日本が行った無謀な戦争に起因している以上、未完のままでいいはずはない。

The Unfinished Aftermath of the War

Column

Japan's defeat in World War II brought unprecedented devastation, and the postwar reparations and settlement process became a massive and complex issue, far from ideal and still unresolved.

The formal postwar settlement between nations was largely concluded with the 1951 San Francisco Peace Treaty. Due to the lessons learned from the harsh reparations after World War I, which contributed to the rise of Nazism, and Cold War dynamics, Japan was spared excessive reparations from the U.S. and European powers. However, treaties with the Soviet Union and others were deferred and the issue of reparations with Asian countries and diplomatic relations to be addressed later.

Territorial disputes, particularly with the Soviet Union over the Northern Territories, remain unresolved. Japan's colonial invasions and occupation of countries like China and Korea have left deep scars, including unresolved compensation and ethnic tensions. The issue of reparations with North Korea is also pending.

Beyond external reparations, the compensation for Japanese citizens' suffering was another complex challenge. The repatriation of around 6.6 million Japanese citizens from overseas was marked by immense hardship. Property confiscated abroad was never compensated, and around 60,000 Japanese nationals were detained in Siberia by the Soviet Union, with many perishing. This issue was long neglected.

In 1981, as memories of the war began to fade, investigations into the descendants of Japanese orphans left in Manchuria began, revealing the depth of unresolved trauma. The recovery of remains of those who died in the southern islands and other regions has also had slow progress.

Domestic civilians affected by air raids and wartime damages still await compensation, while military personnel have been compensated. The government has argued that civilians must endure, rejecting repeated legal challenges for compensation.

The unresolved issues of territorial disputes, colonial legacies, and civilian compensation are difficult to solve. Given that these issues stem from Japan's reckless war, they should not be left unresolved.

残留孤児が祖国日本で肉親捜し
Overseas Japanese war orphans seek blood relatives in their home country

1981（昭和56）年3月2日、祖国日本で肉親捜しをするため北京空港を出発する中国残留日本人孤児たち。終戦による混乱期の旧満州（中国東北部）で家族と生き別れ、中国人に育てられた孤児47人が、初めて集団で一時帰国した。滞在中に身元が判明したのは26人。これまでに国から認定されて永住帰国したのは2024年9月時点で2557人。

Japanese orphans left behind in China after the war departed Beijing Airport in search of blood relatives living in Japan on March 2, 1981. Forty-seven Japanese orphaned by separation from their families in the confusion and anarchy that followed the end of the war in former Manchuria (present-day northeast China), then raised by Chinese families, returned as a group to Japan for the first time. Twenty-six confirmed their Japanese identity during their stay. As of September 2024, the Japanese government has authorized 2,557 Japanese orphans overseas for permanent residence in Japan.

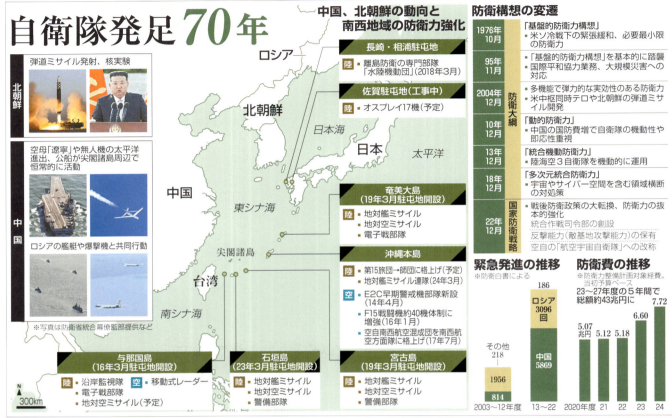

第3章：混迷の時代

　ソ連・東欧共産圏の崩壊と冷戦の終結は、核戦争の脅威からの解放と世界平和の実現に大きく近づくと思わせた。しかしそれは幻想に過ぎなかった。米国、西欧先進国の価値観押しつけと支配に反発する、世界の宗教的、民族的勢力は冷戦のタガが外れた影響もあって、各地で地域紛争やテロを活発化させた。

　日本も他人事では済まされなくなった。1991年の湾岸戦争では国際社会から日本の「目に見える」貢献が求められ、自衛隊初の海外派遣となるペルシャ湾での機雷除去活動、そして国連平和維持活動（PKO）への部隊参加に踏み切る決断がなされた。国内では軍事を含めた国際貢献について、憲法との整合性をめぐっても議論が戦わされるようになった。

　テロの嵐は米中枢同時テロ（2001年）を生み、イスラム過激派と呼ばれる勢力は世界中の各地でテロを繰り返した。2010年代に入ると中国の覇権主義的行動が目立つようになり、ロシアも米欧の結束力、抑止力の弱化を見越したようにウクライナ侵攻に示されるソ連時代の勢力圏回復に踏み出した。

　ロシア、中国などは力による現状変更を目指しているように見え、北朝鮮、イランといった欧米主導の秩序に挑戦する勢力も加わって「新冷戦」ともいわれる現状を示している。核兵器による威嚇も頻繁に耳にするに至った。

　日本でも平和国家を前提とした「戦後」から、既に「新しい戦前」に入ったのではないかと懸念の声も聞かれる。

Chapter 3：An Era of Turmoil

　The collapse of the Soviet Union and the end of the Cold War promised peace but revealed new conflicts. Global tensions rose as opposition to Western dominance fueled terrorism and regional wars.

　Japan, pressured to contribute, deployed the Self-Defense Forces overseas for the first time during the Gulf War and joined UN peacekeeping operations, sparking domestic debates on constitutionality.

　The 9/11 attacks unleashed waves of terrorism by Islamic extremists, while the 2010s saw China assert its dominance and Russia invade Ukraine, seeking to reclaim Soviet-era influence. These actions, alongside challenges from North Korea and Iran, have drawn comparison to a "new Cold War," with frequent nuclear threats.

　Some in Japan now fear that the country has moved from a "postwar" era of peace to a "new prewar" period, amid growing instability.

米海兵隊員が嘉手納から中東へ出発
Marines departed Kadena for the Middle East

1991(平成3)年1月11日、沖縄県の米軍嘉手納基地で、米軍がチャーターしたジャンボ機に乗り込む在沖縄海兵隊員。湾岸危機が高まる中、約340人がサウジアラビアに向けて出発した。90年8月にイラクが隣国のクウェートに侵攻、首都を制圧した。米国中心の多国籍軍が91年1月17日、イラクを大規模空爆作戦で攻撃、湾岸戦争となった。多国籍軍は2月24日にクウェート、イラク南部での地上戦を始め、圧倒的な攻撃でクウェートを奪回した。

Marines stationed in Okinawa board a jumbo jet chartered by the US military at Kadena Air Base, Okinawa, January 11, 1991. Amid the crisis in the Persian Gulf, some 340 Marines departed for Saudi Arabia. In August 1990, Iraq invaded neighboring Kuwait and took control of its capital city. The Gulf War began when a multinational force led by the US commenced a large-scale air offensive on Iraq on January 17, 1991. The allied coalition began a ground offensive in southern Iraq on February 24 and recaptured Kuwait with overwhelming firepower.

発射された巡航ミサイル「トマホーク」
Tomahawk cruise missile launched

1991（平成3）年1月18日未明、湾岸戦争が始まり、ペルシャ湾に展開している米戦艦ウィスコンシンからイラクの目標に向けて発射された巡航ミサイル「トマホーク」。湾岸戦争ではトマホークと地対空ミサイル「パトリオット」が初めて実戦で発射され、敵のレーダーに映りにくい技術を採用したF117ステルス戦闘爆撃機も活躍。多国籍軍がハイテク兵器を駆使した攻撃で圧倒的勝利を収めた。（ロイター）

The Gulf War began early in the morning of January 18, 1991, when the battleship USS Wisconsin deployed to the Persian Gulf launched Tomahawk cruise missiles toward targets in Iraq. The Gulf War saw the first wartime use of Tomahawk missiles, Patriot intercept missiles, and F-117 stealth fighter planes designed with the technology to evade the enemy's radar. By deploying such high-tech weaponry, the multinational coalition achieved overwhelming victory. (Reuters)

横須賀から海自掃海部隊出発
JMSDF unit departs Yokosuka

1991（平成3）年4月26日、神奈川県の海上自衛隊横須賀基地で行われた「ペルシャ湾掃海派遣部隊」の出発式。湾岸戦争の戦後貢献策として掃海部隊の6隻が、計約510人を乗せ横須賀などからペルシャ湾に向けて出港した。24日の安全保障会議と臨時閣議で正式に派遣が決まった。湾岸戦争終結まで、日本の目立った人的貢献はなかった。資金面では計130億㌦を支援したが、国際社会からは「小切手外交」と批判された。

"Maritime Self-Defense Force Persian Gulf minesweeping unit" departure ceremony held at the Japan Maritime SDF Yokosuka Naval Base, Kanagawa Prefecture, April 26, 1991. The six vessels of the minesweeping unit, dispatched to assist in postwar recovery of the Persian Gulf, left port from Yokosuka for the Gulf with around 510 crew members. The dispatch of the unit was officially decided by the National Security Council and an extraordinary Cabinet meeting on April 24. Japan did not provide any particular manpower until the conclusion of the Gulf War. Financially, it provided financial support totaling $13 billion, but this was criticized by the international community as "checkbook diplomacy".

ペルシャ湾入りした海自掃海部隊
JMSDF minesweeping unit enters the Persian Gulf

1991(平成3)年5月26日、ペルシャ湾入りし、アラブ首長国連邦のドバイへ向かう海上自衛隊の掃海部隊。先頭は掃海母艦「はやせ」。湾岸戦争でイラクが敷設した機雷除去と処理が目的。訓練、親善訪問、南極観測などを除いて自衛隊の本格的な海外派遣は初めて。部隊は6月5日から掃海作業を開始、約3カ月間に機雷計34個を爆破処理したほか、クウェート沖で船舶の安全航路拡幅に当たった。

The JMSDF minesweeping unit entered the waters of the Persian Gulf en route to Dubai, United Arab Emirates, on May 26, 1991. Leading the fleet was minesweeper Hayase. The unit's purpose was to remove mines laid by Iraq during the Gulf War. It was the first genuine overseas dispatch of the SDF, excluding training, goodwill visits, and Antarctic research expeditions. The unit commenced minesweeping operations on June 5, and over the next three months, it detonated 34 mines in total, as well as expanding the safety margins for shipping in the waters off Kuwait.

At the Special Parliamentary Committee on International Peacekeeping Operations, Chair Yoshiro Hayashi (center right), who declared question time to be over, was pressed by committee members from the Socialist and Communist parties holding signs aloft with phrases such as "question time continues" and "questions already submitted", June 11, 1992. The Act on Cooperation with United Nations Peacekeeping Operations (PKO) and Other Operations (The International Peace Cooperation Act) and the Act on Dispatchment of the Japan Disaster Relief Team were passed by the House of Councillors on June 9. The Acts were approved that day by the Committee with support from the LDP, Komeito, and Democratic Socialist Party members, making sure that the Acts would be established as law. The International Peace Cooperation Act, which opened the way to genuine international engagements by the SDF, caused fierce ongoing battles between government parties and the opposition over the interpretation of the Constitution and other aspects.

PKO協力法案の質疑打ち切りで抗議
Curtailment of questions about the International Peace Cooperation Act

1992(平成4)年6月11日、衆院国際平和協力特別委員会で、質疑打ち切りを宣言した林義郎委員長(中央右)に「質疑続行」「質問通告済」などと書いた紙を広げて詰め寄る社会、共産両党の委員。国連平和維持活動(PKO)協力法案と、国際緊急援助隊派遣法改正案は9日に参院を通過、この日の委員会で自民、公明、民社3党の賛成で可決され、成立が確実となった。自衛隊の本格的な海外派遣に道を開くPKO協力法案は、憲法解釈などをめぐり与野党の激しい攻防が続いた。

PKO協力法に市民グループが抗議
Citizen's groups oppose the International Peace Cooperation Law

1992(平成4)年6月15日、国連平和維持活動(PKO)協力法に反対して、国会の衆院議員面会所前に詰めかけ抗議する市民グループ。同法はこの日、社会党、社民連両党議員欠席のまま開かれた衆院本会議で自民、公明、民社3党などの賛成で可決、成立した。共産党は反対した。自衛隊は54年の発足以来、初めて本格的な海外活動を展開するための法的根拠を持つことになった。

Citizen's groups crowded the meeting area of the Diet to oppose the Act on Cooperation with United Nations PKO and Other Operations, June 15, 1992. On this day, the Act was approved and passed into law by the LDP, Komeito, and Democratic Socialist Party during a plenary session of the House of Representatives held in the absence of the Socialist Party and the Socialist Democratic Federation. The Communist Party opposed the Acts. It provided the legal basis for the first genuine overseas deployment of the SDF since its establishment in 1954.

見送りの人に帽子振る派遣隊員
Dispatched unit wave caps at well-wishers

1992(平成4)年9月17日、広島県呉市の海上自衛隊呉基地で、カンボジアに向かう輸送艦「みうら」から見送りの人たちに帽子を振る派遣隊員。国連平和維持活動(PKO)協力法に基づく海外派遣で、施設部隊用の車両や隊員たちの食料などを輸送した。自衛隊の海外派遣は、訓練目的などを除いては海自ペルシャ湾掃海部隊に続くもので、PKO協力法を受けての派遣は初めて。

At the Maritime Self-Defense Force Kure Naval Base in Kure City, Hiroshima Prefecture, members of the dispatch unit aboard the transport ship Miura bound for Cambodia wave their caps as well-wishers see them off, September 17, 1992. Under the International Peace Cooperation Law, their overseas mission involved transporting vehicles for the engineering corps and food for the unit. Other than for training purposes, this overseas deployment of the SDF was the first since the Maritime SDF minesweeping unit was dispatched to the Persian Gulf and the first time that the SDF was dispatched under the International Peace Cooperation Law.

PKO部隊が修復工事開始
Peacekeeping unit starts reconstruction

1992（平成4）年10月28日、カンボジア南部タケオの西方で、国連平和維持活動（PKO）に参加している陸上自衛隊の施設部隊が、派遣の主任務である国道3号の修復工事を開始した。個人参加の形で既に活動を始めていた停戦監視に続き、自衛隊の部隊としては初めてのPKOが本格的に始動した。

The engineering unit of the Ground SDF undertook a United Nations peacekeeping operation in the west of Takeo Province, southern Cambodia, October 28, 1992. Its principal mission was to start rebuilding work on National Highway 3. Some members of the SDF were already taking part in ceasefire monitoring, but this marked the first real PKO mission for a whole unit of the SDF.

派遣隊員は宿営地でテント生活
Unit leads life under canvas at camp

1994（平成6）年10月9日、ザイール（現コンゴ）東部ゴマの自衛隊宿営地のテント内で昼食を取る隊員。ルワンダ難民の人道援助を目的に派遣された部隊は医療、給水、防疫が主な任務で、国連平和維持活動（PKO）協力法に基づく自衛隊初の海外人道救援活動。宿営地周辺では夜間、頻繁に銃声が聞こえるなど隊員らは緊張の中での生活を強いられた。

SDF personnel eating lunch in their tent at the SDF camp in Goma, eastern Zaire (present-day Democratic Republic of the Congo), October 9, 1994. This was the first humanitarian mission for the SDF under the International Peace Cooperation Law, with the primary task of providing humanitarian aid to Rwandan refugees, including medical assistance, water, and infection prevention. Daily life was tense for the unit as nighttime frequently brought the sound of gunfire in the area around the camp.

文民警察官が武装集団に襲われ死亡
Civilian police officer killed by armed group

1993(平成5)年5月5日、バンコクのドンムアン空軍基地に移送された文民警察官、高田晴行警部補のひつぎ。高田警部補は国連平和維持活動(PKO)でカンボジアに派遣されていたが4日、オランダ軍の護衛付きでカンボジア北西部の国道を移動中に武装集団に襲われ死亡した。同行していた他の日本人警察官4人も重軽傷。日本人は防弾チョッキを着けていなかった。文民警察官は、地元警察の指導などが主な任務。

The coffin of civilian police officer Haruyuki Takata, Don Muang Royal Thai Air Base, Bangkok, May 5, 1993. Takata died during a UN peacekeeping operation when an armed group attacked the Dutch Army Convoy he was working with along a national road in northwest Cambodia on May 4. Four other Japanese police officers accompanying the convoy were also injured. The Japanese officers were not wearing bulletproof vests at the time. One primary task of civilian police officers was to offer instructions to local police.

海上自衛隊観艦式の村山首相
Prime Minister Murayama attends Maritime SDF fleet review

1994(平成6)年10月16日、神奈川県沖の相模湾で行われた海上自衛隊の観艦式で、護衛艦「しらね」の艦上から海上パレードを観閲する村山富市首相。6月29日、首相指名選挙で自民、社会、新党さきがけの3党が推す村山社会党委員長が第81代首相に選出された。国会答弁で社会党の基本政策を大転換、自衛隊を合憲と認め、日米安保条約を必要、不可欠とした。

Prime Minister Tomiichi Murayama watched a fleet review from the JS Shirane destroyer on Sagami Bay, Kanagawa Prefecture, October 16, 1994. Socialist Party leader Murayama was elected the 81st Prime Minister by a coalition of three Diet parties, the LDP, the Socialist Party, and New Party Sakigake on June 29. In response to questions in the Diet, the Prime Minister transformed the basic policies of the Socialist Party, accepting the SDF as aligned with the Constitution and the indispensability of the Japan-US Security Treaty.

米兵暴行事件に抗議し沖縄県民総決起大会
Protest against rape committed by a US soldier in Okinawa

1995(平成7)年10月21日、沖縄県の宜野湾市で開かれた、米兵による少女暴行事件に抗議する沖縄県民総決起大会。主催者発表で約8万5千人が参加、本土復帰後の沖縄では空前の大規模集会となった。大会では米軍基地の整理縮小と日米地位協定見直しなどを求める決議を採択、米軍基地の重圧を日米両政府に訴えた。

The meeting protesting the rape of an elementary school girl by a US soldier was held in Ginowan, Okinawa Prefecture, October 21, 1995. According to the organizers, it was attended by some 85,000 people, making it easily the largest crowd to gather since the reversion of Okinawa in 1972. The protest meeting adopted a resolution calling for the reduction of US military bases and a review of the Japan-US Status of Forces Agreement and appealed to the Japanese and US governments to remove pressure on US military bases.

米中枢同時テロでツインタワー炎上
Twin towers in flames by terrorist attacks on 9/11

2001(平成13)年9月11日、テロリストに乗っ取られた旅客機2機が突っ込み炎上する米ニューヨークの世界貿易センターのツインタワー。この後、2棟とも崩壊した。ニューヨークやワシントンなど米国の中枢を狙った同時テロでは旅客機4機がハイジャックされ、日本人24人を含む約3千人が犠牲になった。ブッシュ(子)政権は国際テロ組織アルカイダの犯行と断定、指導者のウサマ・ビンラディン容疑者をかくまったとして10月7日、アフガニスタンのタリバン政権への報復空爆を開始した。(ロイター)

The twin towers of the World Trade Center, New York, in flames after two passenger jets were hijacked by terrorists and flown into the buildings, September 11, 2001. The towers would soon collapse. The synchronized terror attacks on New York, Washington, and other core areas of the US involved the hijacking of four passenger jets, resulting in the death of approximately 3,000 people, including 24 Japanese nationals. The administration of George W. Bush determined that the global terrorist group al-Qaeda was responsible and launched retaliatory airstrikes against the Taliban regime in Afghanistan on October 7 for allegedly harboring its leader, Osama bin Laden. (Reuters)

米英軍イラク攻撃開始
US and UK launch war on Iraq

2003（平成15）年3月21日、米英軍によるイラクの首都バグダッドへの空爆で炎上する政権中枢施設。米国のブッシュ（子）大統領は20日、イラクのフセイン政権が大量破壊兵器を保有し、国際テロ組織アルカイダを支援していると主張しイラクへの攻撃を開始した。4月にフセイン政権は崩壊したが、大量破壊兵器は見つからず、テロや宗派間抗争が激化。米軍の駐留は11年12月まで約8年9カ月続き、武装勢力のテロや米軍の攻撃などでイラク市民11万人以上が犠牲になった。（ロイター）

Central government buildings of the Iraqi capital Baghdad in flames after air strikes by the US and UK, March 21 2003. US President George W. Bush launched the attack on Iraq, claiming that Iraqi President Saddam Hussein possessed weapons of mass destruction and had provided support to Al-Qaida. The Hussein regime fell in April, but no weapons of mass destruction were found and terrorism and sectarian conflict worsened. The US occupation continued until December 2011, or 8 years and 9 months, at the sacrifice of more than 110,000 Iraqis killed by terrorist attacks by armed groups and US military operations. (Reuters)

進軍する米部隊と炎上するタンクローリー
Advancing US troops and a tanker in flames

2003(平成15)年4月6日、イラクの首都バグダッドに展開する米軍部隊の前方で炎上するイラクのタンクローリー。米英軍は3月20日、限定空爆で軍事作戦を開始、地上軍もクウェートから進攻し、4月9日には首都を制圧した。この写真は米陸軍部隊に従軍した共同通信記者が撮影した。イラク戦争では約800人の記者が米英軍に従軍、歴史上メディアが最も報道した戦争の一つとされる。

An Iraqi fuel tanker on fire in front of US troops advancing across the Iraqi capital, Baghdad, April 6, 2003. The US and UK armies launched a campaign of limited air strikes on March 20, with ground forces invading from Kuwait, taking control of the capital on April 9. This photograph was taken by a Kyodo News reporter embedded with a US Army unit. Around 800 journalists were embedded with US and UK troops in the Iraq war, making it one of the most widely covered wars in history.

復興支援で陸自部隊がイラク入り
Ground SDF unit enters Iraq to assist reconstruction

2004(平成16)年2月8日、クウェートから国境を越え、イラク入りする陸上自衛隊本隊第1陣の車列。機関銃などで武装した軽装甲機動車や装輪装甲車による自前の警備で、トラックや建設用の重機を積んだトレーラーが連なった。イラク復興支援特別措置法による派遣で、南部サマワでの人道復興支援が任務。同法は前年7月に成立、自衛隊の活動は、現に戦闘が行われておらず、今後も戦闘が行われないと認められる「非戦闘地域」に限るとされた。

The first unit of the Ground SDF crosses the border in convoy from Kuwait into Iraq, February 8, 2004. They secured themselves with light armored vehicles armed with machine guns and armored personnel carriers, as they transported trucks and construction equipment on trailers. The mission of humanitarian reconstruction support in Samawah, southern Iraq, was carried out under the Act on Special Measures Concerning Humanitarian Relief and Reconstruction Work and Security Assistance in Iraq. The law was passed in July 2003 and restricted SDF activities to "non-battle zones" where no fighting was taking place and where it could be assured that no fighting would occur in the future.

海自補給艦が米英加3艦に洋上給油
Maritime SDF supply ship provides refueling for US, UK, and Canadian ships

2004（平成16）年3月10日、インド洋北部のアラビア海で米、英、カナダの3艦船に洋上給油作業をする海上自衛隊の補給艦「ときわ」（中央）。01年12月からテロ対策特別措置法に基づく米軍への協力支援活動の一環として米艦船への燃料給油が行われた。海自のインド洋での給油活動は、改正新テロ対策特別措置法の期限切れにより、10年1月で終了。米中枢同時テロを受けた「テロとの戦い」への協力で、自衛隊初の「戦時下」派遣となった給油活動は約8年で終了した。

Maritime SDF supply vessel Tokiwa (center) refueled an American ship, a British ship, and a Canadian ship in the northern Indian Ocean, March 10, 2004. Under the Anti-Terrorism Special Measures Act, Japan provided refueling for US ships as part of its cooperation with the US military from December 2001. Maritime SDF refueling activities on the Indian Ocean were curtailed in January 2010 when the Revised Anti-Terrorism Special Measures Act expired. The SDF's first "wartime" dispatch, a refueling mission to assist the War on Terror following the 9/11 terrorist attacks, ended after some eight years.

自衛隊チームがフィリピンで医療活動
SDF team undertakes medical relief in the Philippines

2013（平成25）年11月24日、台風被災地、フィリピン・セブ島北部で、子どもを診察する自衛隊の国際緊急援助隊本隊の医療チーム。台風30号ではレイテ島の最大都市タクロバンなどが壊滅的な被害を受け、フィリピンの死者・行方不明者は約7400人。日本は国際緊急援助隊として自衛隊員1180人を派遣、医療や救援物資の輸送などを担った。

The medical unit of the SDF Japan Disaster Relief Team examined children in northern Cebu, Philippines, in the wake of a typhoon disaster on November 24, 2013. Typhoon No. 30 caused catastrophic damage to Tacloban, the biggest city on Leyte Island, leaving some 7,400 Filipinos dead or missing. The Japan Disaster Relief Team included the dispatch of 1,180 SDF personnel, who offered medical assistance and transportation of aid supplies.

イラク・サマワに陸自女性隊員
Female SDF personnel in Samawah, Iraq

2004（平成16）年3月21日、イラク南部サマワの自衛隊の仮宿営地で銃を持ち整列する陸上自衛隊の女性隊員。女性隊員のイラク入りは初めてで、海外派遣への女性自衛官参加は東ティモール国連平和維持活動（PKO）に続き2例目。サマワでは医療や通信、輸送業務、対外調整などを担当。

Armed female personnel of a Ground SDF unit lined up at the SDF camp in Samawah, southern Iraq, March 21, 2004. They were the first female troops in Iraq, making this the second overseas dispatch of female SDF forces after the peacekeeping mission to East Timor. Their tasks included medicine, telecommunications, transportation, and external relations.

上皇ご夫妻がサイパン訪問
Retired Emperor and Emperess visit Saipan

2005(平成17)年6月28日、太平洋戦争の犠牲者を慰霊するため米自治領サイパンを訪問、多くの日本人が身を投げたスーサイドクリフから海を見つめられる上皇ご夫妻(当時天皇、皇后両陛下)。戦後50年に当たる1995年に長崎、広島、沖縄、東京都慰霊堂を訪れたのに続き、戦後60年のこの年、初の海外慰霊の旅としてサイパン訪問が実現した。戦後70年の2015年には、激戦地となった西太平洋の島国パラオも訪問。

On a visit to the US territory of Saipan to commemorate the victims of the Pacific War, the Retired Emperor and Emperess (then the Emperor and Empress) looked out to sea from Suicide Cliff, where a large number of Japanese leaped to their deaths, June 28, 2005. On the 50th anniversary of the end of the war in 1995, they visited Nagasaki, Hiroshima, Okinawa, and the Tokyo Memorial Hall. On the 60th anniversary, in 2005, they traveled to Saipan as the first overseas commemoration trip. On the 70th anniversary, in 2015, they visited Palau in the western Pacific, a site of fierce battles.

イラク派遣隊員と握手する小泉首相
Prime Minister Koizumi shakes hands w th soldiers heading to Iraq

2004(平成16)年5月8日、北海道の航空自衛隊千歳基地で、政府専用機に乗り込む陸上自衛隊イラク派遣の第2次部隊の隊員一人一人と握手する小泉純一郎首相(右下)。イラク復興支援特別措置法に基づき04年1月〜06年7月、陸自隊員延べ約5500人が南部サマワに派遣された。空自は04〜08年、クウェートを拠点に当初はサマワ近郊に物資を輸送。陸自撤収後は首都バグダッドなどに活動範囲を広げ、多国籍軍兵士も運んだ。

Prime Minister Junichiro Koizumi (lower right) shakes hands with each member of the Second Unit of the SDF Iraq dispatch as they board a government jet at JASDF Chitose Air Base, Hokkaido, May 8, 2004. Under the Act on Special Measures Concerning Humanitarian Relief and Reconstruction Work and Security Assistance in Iraq, from January 2004 to July 2006, some 5,500 Ground SDF personnel were dispatched to Samawah, southern Iraq. From 2004 to 2008, the Air SDF transported supplies to the outskirts of Samawah from a hub in Kuwait. Following the withdrawal of the Ground SDF, they expanded the scope of their activities to the capital, Baghdad and also transported soldiers of the multinational coalition.

ソマリア沖で海自護衛艦が船舶警護
Maritime SDF ship escorts shipping off Somalia

2009（平成21）年6月6日、アフリカ東部ソマリア沖のアデン湾で商船を警護する海上自衛隊の護衛艦「さみだれ」（手前）。ソマリア沖の海賊対策で、自衛隊法に基づく海上警備行動が発令され、航行する船舶の警護任務に就く。アデン湾は、スエズ運河を経由しアジアと欧州を結ぶ重要な海上交通路。08年ごろから周辺海域で海賊被害が顕在化してからは各国が海軍部隊を派遣するようになった。

The Maritime SDF destroyer Samidare escorted merchant shipping in the Gulf of Aden, off Somalia, eastern Africa, June 6, 2009 (foreground). She was deployed under the Self-Defense Forces Act to combat piracy off the coast of Somalia, with the mission to escort ships in their passage through the area. The Gulf of Aden is a major maritime route connecting Asia and Europe via the Suez Canal. Due to the presence of pirates in the surrounding waters, navies from around the world have dispatched missions to the area since 2008.

アフガン支援の中村哲さん
Tetsu Nakamura, Afghan aid legend

2010（平成22）年2月8日、アフガニスタン東部ジャララバード近郊で開かれた農業用水路の完工式で、州知事に抱き上げられる中村哲さん。福岡市の非政府組織「ペシャワール会」現地代表の医師で、アフガニスタンやパキスタンで貧困層の医療や農業の支援に取り組んだ。現地での信頼も厚くアフガン政府から名誉市民権も授与された。過激派組織が活動する地域で、危険と隣り合わせの支援活動を続けたが、19年12月4日、武装集団に銃撃され、73歳で命を落とした。

Tetsu Nakamura hoisted aloft by the Governor of Nangarhar province at the completion ceremony of agricultural canals on the outskirts of Jalalabad, eastern Afghanistan, February 8, 2010. As head of the non-profit organization Peace Japan Medical Services, based in Fukuoka, Nakamura was committed to medical and agricultural assistance to the poor of Afghanistan and Pakistan. Highly trusted in the region, he was awarded honorary citizenship by the Afghan government. Nakamura had long worked in areas where extremist groups operated, but on December 4, 2019, at the age of 73, he was shot and killed by an armed group.

海自P3Cが海賊監視活動
Maritime SDF P3C on anti-piracy patrol

2010（平成22）年1月19日、海賊被害が増え続けるソマリア沖のアデン湾で、上空から警戒監視活動をする海上自衛隊のP3C哨戒機（中央）と航行する商船（下）。海自P3C部隊は活動当初、アフリカ東部のジブチ空港の米軍施設を借りて活動拠点としていた。政府は活動の長期化を見据え11年6月、ジブチ空港北側に新たな拠点を開設。借り上げた土地に司令部庁舎や宿舎、P3Cの整備用格納庫、隊員のための体育館などを建設した。自衛隊の海外初の本格拠点。

The maritime SDF P-3C patrol aircraft (C) flew over a merchant ship (below) as it carried out surveillance activities from the air over the Gulf of Aden, near Somalia where pirate attacks continued to increase, January 19, 2010. The SDF P-3C unit was initially based in a US military facility in Djibouti Airport, eastern Africa. In preparation for a longer mission, the Japanese government established a new base on the north side of Djibouti Airport in June 2011. On leased land, a headquarters building, a dormitory, a hangar for P-3C maintenance, and a gymnasium for the corps were erected. It was the first fully-fledged overseas base for the SDF.

東日本大震災の津波被災地を捜索
Search and rescue in tsunami-stricken area during Great East Japan Earthquake disaster

2011（平成23）年3月14日、東日本大震災の津波で住宅が流された宮城県東松島市の沿岸部を捜索する自衛隊員と消防隊員。東日本大震災の自衛隊の災害派遣は3月11日から8月31日にかけ、延べ1千万人超が投入された。震災直後、米軍も空母ロナルド・レーガンを中心とする艦隊を東北地方の太平洋沖へ急派、「トモダチ作戦」としてヘリコプターによる行方不明者の捜索活動や支援物資の輸送、復旧作業に従事した。

SDF personnel and firefighters searched along the coast of Higashimatsushima City, Miyagi Prefecture, where homes were washed away by a tsunami in the Great East Japan Earthquake disaster, March 14, 2011. Between March 11 and August 31, more than 10 million personnel were dispatched on the SDF mission following the Great East Japan Earthquake. Immediately after the earthquake, the US urgently dispatched a fleet led by the aircraft carrier USS Ronald Reagan to the Pacific coast of the Tohoku region to search for missing people by helicopter, to transport relief supplies, and to assist recovery under "Operation Tomodachi".

オスプレイで日米共同訓練
Joint Japan-US Osprey training

2013(平成25)年2月13日、米カリフォルニア州の海兵隊基地で行われた日米共同訓練で、海兵隊員(右の2人)と共に輸送機MV22オスプレイから降り立った陸上自衛隊員。自衛隊員が訓練でオスプレイに搭乗するのは初。陸自はV22オスプレイ17機を導入、24年6月に千葉県の陸自木更津駐屯地への暫定配備が完了。最終的に、建設中の佐賀空港隣接の新駐屯地へ移駐する予定。オスプレイは米軍による開発段階から事故やトラブルが相次ぎ、安全性が懸念されている。

US Marines (the two soldiers on the right) and Ground SDF personnel disembarked from an MV-22 Osprey transport plane during joint Japan-US training at a Marine Corps camp in California, February 13, 2013. This training was the first time SDF personnel had ever flown in an Osprey. The SDF has now purchased 17 V-22 Ospreys and completed their provisional deployment to JGSDF Camp Kisarazu, Chiba Prefecture in June 2024. Eventually, the aircrafts will be transferred to the new stationing post currenty under construction adjacent to Saga Airport. The Osprey planes have been plagued by accidents and incidents since the development stage with the US military and safety remains a concern.

リズムに乗って安保関連法に抗議
Marching to rhythmic music in protest of the security bills

2015（平成27）年9月11日、国会議事堂前でリズムに乗って安全保障関連法案に反対する大学生らのグループ「SEALDs（シールズ）」のメンバーら。シールズは、憲法解釈を変更し集団的自衛権行使を容認した政権に抗議する若者が創設。交流サイト（SNS）を通じて情報を発信、チラシやパンフレットは、中身だけでなくデザインにこだわった。斬新なスタイルが共感を呼び、参加者数は飛躍的に増えた。

Outside the National Diet Building, Tokyo, members of the university student group SEALDs marched to rhythmic music in opposition to the package of security bills on September 11, 2015. SEALDs was established by students opposed to the Abe government's acceptance of the exercise of the right of collective self-defense by reinterpreting the Constitution. The group would stay up to date via social media and take great care over the design as well as the content of their posters and pamphlets. The innovative approach resonated, and the group dramatically increased in size.

国会議事堂正門前で安保関連法に抗議
Protest in front of the National Diet Building over security bills

2015（平成27）年8月30日、参院で審議中の安全保障関連法案に反対する抗議行動で、国会議事堂正門前の道路を埋め尽くした大勢の人たち。主催者によると全国200カ所以上で同様のデモや集会を実施。安全保障関連法は、安倍政権が閣議決定した憲法解釈変更による集団的自衛権の行使容認や、他国軍への後方支援拡大などを盛り込んだ法律。密接な関係にある他国が攻撃を受けて日本の存立が脅かされる場合を「存立危機事態」とし、他に適当な手段がないなどの要件を満たせば集団的自衛権を行使できると定めた。

Thousands of people filled the road in front of the National Diet Building to protest the package of security bills under consideration by the House of Councilors on August 30, 2015. According to organizers, demonstrations were held simultaneously in over 200 locations around Japan. The security bills incorporate acceptance of the exercise of the right of collective self-defense via a new interpretation of the Constitution as decided by the Cabinet of the Abe administration, as well as expansion of rear-area support to other countries' militaries. They permit the use of force by the SDF in the event that a country in a close relationship with Japan is under armed attack and Japan's existence is threatened as a result if conditions are met and there are no other appropriate responses.

広島で被爆者抱き締めるオバマ米大統領
US President Obama hugs hibakusha in Hiroshima

2016（平成28）年5月27日、現職米大統領として初めて広島市の平和記念公園を訪れ、被爆者の森重昭さんを抱き締めるオバマ大統領。森さんは広島で被爆死した米兵捕虜12人の身元特定に尽力した。オバマ氏は被爆者らを前にした演説で「（核保有国は）核兵器なき世界を追求する勇気を持たなければならない」と決意を表明した。原爆投下の是非には言及せず、謝罪はしなかった。
President Barack Obama hugged Mr. Shigeaki Mori, a hibakusha (survivor of the atomic bomb) during the first visit by a sitting US president to Peace Memorial Park, Hiroshima, May 27, 2016. Mori worked for decades on investigating the fate of 12 US prisoners of war who perished in the bombing of Hiroshima. Speaking before gathered bomb survivors, Obama expressed his resolve that "Among those nations that hold nuclear stockpiles, we must have the courage to pursue a world without them". He did not mention whether the bombing was right or wrong, nor did he make any apology.

南スーダンPKOで警戒する陸自隊員
Ground SDF personnel on patrol during PKO in South Sudan

2016(平成28)年11月14日、南スーダン・ジュバの国連平和維持活動(PKO)施設内の作業現場で警戒活動をする陸上自衛隊員。3月に安全保障関連法が施行され、南スーダンに派遣されている自衛隊部隊には12月から、襲われた国連要員や他国部隊を助ける「駆け付け警護」と、武装集団の襲撃に他国軍と共に対処する「宿営地の共同防衛」の新任務が付与された。

Ground SDF personnel carried out a patrol around a workshop in a United Nations peacekeeping operation(PKO) compound during their peacekeeping operation in Juba, South Sudan, November 14, 2016. With the package of security laws coming into force in March, the Ground SDF unit dispatched to South Sudan was tasked with the additional duties of coming to the aid of geographically distant peacekeeping units or United Nations personnel under attack, and "joint protection of camps" whereby SDF personnel would repel attacks by armed groups together with other nations' militaries.

US President Donald Trump issued instructions to Japanese and US personnel during an inspection of the JS Kaga destroyer docked at the Japan Maritime SDF Yokosuka Naval Base, Kanagawa Prefecture, May 28, 2019. To the right is Prime Minister Shinzo Abe. The event was intended to underline the strength of the alliance between Japan and the US.

海自護衛艦でトランプ米大統領が訓示
US President Trump issues instructions aboard Maritime SDF ship

2019（令和元）年5月28日、神奈川県横須賀市の海上自衛隊横須賀基地に停泊する護衛艦「かが」を視察し、日米の隊員に訓示するトランプ米大統領。右は安倍晋三首相。日米の強固な同盟関係をアピールした。

伊江島で米海兵隊訓練
US Marines train on Ie Island

2020（令和2）年10月7日、沖縄県・伊江島の米軍伊江島補助飛行場（伊江村）に到着した輸送機オスプレイから降り、訓練する海兵隊員。太平洋戦争当時「東洋一の規模」と言われた日本軍の飛行場があった伊江島は沖縄戦の激戦地で、村民の半数に当たる約1500人が犠牲になった。伊江島補助飛行場は、1945年4月に米軍が上陸と同時に占領、日本軍自らが破壊した滑走路を修復、拡張する形で使用を始めた。同飛行場は伊江村の面積の約35％を占める。

US Marines disembarked from the Osprey transport aircraft on a training exercise at the Ie Shima Auxiliary Airfield, Iejima Village, Okinawa Prefecture, October 7, 2020. Iejima (then anglicized as Ie Shima) was a Japanese military airfield considered the largest in Asia during the Pacific War and the site of intense fighting during the invasion of Okinawa, with around 1,500 islanders killed, more than half of the resident population. The Ie Shima Auxiliary Airfield was captured when the US military landed in April 1945, and they began to use it once they had repaired the sabotage to the runway done by the departing Japanese military and extended it. The airfield accounts for around 35% of the land area of the island.

ウクライナへ防弾チョッキ提供
Bulletproof vests to Ukraine

2022（令和4）年3月8日、愛知県の航空自衛隊小牧基地で、KC767空中給油輸送機に積み込まれるウクライナ向け支援物資。政府はこの日、ロシア軍の侵攻を受けるウクライナに防衛装備品である防弾チョッキを提供するため、輸出ルールを定めた「防衛装備移転三原則」の運用指針を改定した。防弾チョッキなど支援物資を積み込んだ自衛隊機は午後11時ごろ、隣国ポーランドに向け出発した。

The Japan Air Self-Defense Force KC-767 refueling tanker was loaded with supplies for Ukraine at JASDF Komaki base, Aichi Prefecture, March 8, 2022. On that day, the government amended the implementation guidelines of the Three Principles on Transfer of Defense Equipment and Technology to enable the supply of bulletproof vests, defined as defense equipment, to Ukraine as it endured the Russian invasion. The Air SDF plane was loaded with supplies, including bulletproof vests, and departed at around 11 pm, bound for Ukraine's neighbor, Poland.

尖閣諸島に中国海警局の船
China Coast Guard ship in Senkaku Islands

2024（令和6）年4月27日、沖縄県・尖閣諸島の魚釣島周辺を航行する中国海警局の船（奥）と海上保安庁の巡視船。尖閣諸島周辺では、領有権を主張する中国の海警局船による領海侵入が常態化。海警局船の大型化、武装化も進んでいる。公船の活動を常態化させることで、領有権を内外にアピールする狙いがあるとみられる。

A Chinese Coast Guard ship (rear) steamed through waters near Uotsuri Island of Senkaku Islands, Okinawa Prefecture, April 27, 2024. The China Coast Guard now routinely enters the waters around the Senkakus, which it claims are Chinese territory. The size of its vessels is growing, and they are increasingly well-armed. It appears that China is promoting its territorial claims through the routine presence of its official vessels in these waters.

ガザの破壊された建物で救助活動
Rescue efforts in rubble of Gaza

2024(令和6)年6月22日、パレスチナ自治区ガザ北部ガザ市で、イスラエルの攻撃を受け破壊された建物で救助活動をする人たち。23年10月7日、ガザのイスラム組織ハマスが越境攻撃でイスラエルの兵士や民間人多数を殺害、拉致。イスラエルは直ちに報復攻撃を開始した。空爆や砲撃に加え、地上侵攻で病院も襲撃し掃討戦を展開。民間人を巻き込んだ甚大な被害に国際社会からは非難の声が上がった。(ロイター)

Rescuers working in the ruins of a building destroyed by an Israeli attack in Gaza City, northern Gaza Strip, June 22, 2024. On October 7, 2023, Gaza's Islamist organization Hamas launched a cross-border attack and killed a large number of soldiers and civilians, as well as taking hostages. Israel immediately began retaliatory attacks. In addition to air raids and artillery fire, it conducted a ground invasion to annihilate Hamas, even including attacks on hospitals. The international community has condemned civilians being killed in the massive destruction. (Reuters)

ミサイル攻撃受けた病院で救助活動
Rescue efforts underway after missile attack on hospital

2024（令和6）年7月8日、ロシアのミサイル攻撃で被害を受けたウクライナ首都キーウ（キエフ）の小児病院で救助活動をする人たち。キーウでは、国内最大の小児病院や産科病院、保育園、大学が攻撃を受けた。ウクライナ当局によると、この日の大規模攻撃では40人以上が死亡し、約200人が負傷。（ロイター）

Rescue efforts are underway at a children's hospital following a Russian missile attack on Kyiv, the capital of Ukraine, July 8, 2024. In Kyiv, the country's largest children's hospital, a maternity hospital, a kindergarten, and a university were attacked. According to Ukrainian authorities, the massive attack killed over 40 people and injured around 200 others. (Reuters)

ガザへの攻撃停止を求めキャンドル集会
Candlelight rally for ceasefire in Gaza

2023(令和5)年11月26日、広島市の原爆ドーム前で開かれたイスラエルによるパレスチナ自治区ガザへの攻撃停止を求める集会。市民らはキャンドルを並べて文字を描き、「ジェノサイド(民族大量虐殺)を止めよう」と訴えた。

People gathered for a solidarity rally calling for Israel to cease its attacks on the Palestinian territory of Gaza held in front of the A-bomb Dome, Hiroshima, November 26, 2023. Attendees lit their candles to form the words, "Stop Genocide in Gaza".

コラム

「核」の戦後80年

　広島と長崎に投下された原爆は20万人もの一般市民の命を奪い、生存者もその後長く苦しみを強いられた。最悪の大量殺りく兵器であることが明白になっても、世界は「国防」「正義」「平和維持」などの名のもとに開発競争と配備拡大に突き進み、実際に使用されるリスクがこれまでになく高まっている。

　米国は原爆製造技術の独占を図ったが、1949年にはソ連が原爆実験に成功、英国、フランスも"核クラブ"の仲間入りをした。さらに強力な水爆実験も米国を先頭に各国が追随し、冷戦を背景とした核兵器開発競争が展開された。

　55年、広島で初の原水爆禁止世界大会が開催され、世界でもバートランド・ラッセルやアインシュタインといった著名な哲学者、科学者をはじめとした反核の動きが盛り上がった。

　60年代に入ると「キューバ危機」を経て核軍縮への動きも始まり、63年8月には米、英、ソにより部分的核実験禁止条約が調印された。しかし中国が64年10月に、インドが74年5月に、それぞれ核実験をするなど核保有国は一気に増え、米ソ両超大国の影響力低下により新秩序構築が課題となった。

　このような流れへの危機感から80年代は世界的に再び反核の機運が盛り上がり、市民レベルの運動も大規模に展開された。90年代、冷戦の終結とソ連の崩壊に伴って核兵器の管理と拡散防止が課題となったが、北朝鮮、イランといった国が核保有に意欲を見せ、テロリストへの核流出も懸念される事態となった。

　2000年以後は中国が核を含めた軍備を急速に拡大させ、北朝鮮が核実験とロケット技術開発を加速させて東アジアをめぐる安保情勢が緊張化した。

　日本では1967年12月に佐藤栄作首相が「非核三原則」を打ち出して国是とされたが、最近になって三原則の見直しや、核保有をめぐる議論を容認する発言などが政府周辺からも出るようになった。ウクライナを侵略したロシアやガザ侵攻のイスラエルなどからは核使用の脅迫が頻繁に聞かれる。

　そうした中で2024年、日本原水爆被害者団体協議会（1956年結成、被団協）がノーベル平和賞を受賞した。

80 Years Since the "Nuclear" Aftermath

Column

The atomic bombings of Hiroshima and Nagasaki killed 200,000 civilians and caused lasting suffering. Despite the clear devastation, the world pursued a dangerous arms race in the name of "national defense" and "peacekeeping," increasing the risk of nuclear war.

The U.S. sought a monopoly on nuclear technology, but by 1949, the Soviet Union, UK, and France developed their own bombs. The Cold War escalated this arms race, with the U.S. leading the development of hydrogen bombs. In 1955, the first World Conference for the Abolition of Nuclear Weapons was held in Hiroshima, gaining support from figures like Bertrand Russell and Albert Einstein. The 1960s saw moves toward nuclear disarmament, but tests by China and India led to a rapid increase in nuclear powers.

In the 1980s, anti-nuclear movements surged, and after the Cold War ended in the 1990s, nuclear non-proliferation became a priority. However, countries like North Korea and Iran began pursuing nuclear weapons, and the threat of nuclear terrorism grew.

Since 2000, China has expanded its military, including nuclear arms, and North Korea has advanced its nuclear capabilities, heightening tensions in East Asia. Japan's Prime Minister Eisaku Sato declared the "Three Non-Nuclear Principles" in 1967, but recent discussions on revising these principles have emerged.

In this context, Japan Confederation of A- and H-Bomb Sufferers Organizations (established in 1956, Nihon Hidankyo) received the Nobel Peace Prize in 2024.

2024(令和6)年12月10日、ノルウェー・オスロで開かれた授賞式で、ノーベル平和賞を贈られた日本原水爆被害者団体協議会(被団協)の代表団。
Members of the Japanese organization Nihon Hidankyo are seen at the City Hall on the occasion of the award ceremony of the Nobel Peace Prize in Oslo, Norway December 10, 2024.

世界の核弾頭数 ストックホルム国際平和研究所の推計（2024年1月）	
ロ シ ア	5580発
米 国	5044
中 国	500
フランス	290
英 国	225
イ ン ド	172
パキスタン	170
イスラエル	90
北 朝 鮮	50
計1万2121発	

	9カ国の核兵器関連支出額 ICANの推計、単位は米ドル（2023年）	
1	米国	515億
2	中国	119億
3	ロシア	83億
4	英国	81億
5	フランス	61億
6	インド	27億
7	イスラエル	11億
8	パキスタン	10億
9	北朝鮮	8.56億
	計	914億

エピローグ：戦火の子どもたち

　戦争がどんな理由で、どこで戦われようが常に最大の被害者となるのが子どもたちだ。被害の内容は殺害、負傷にとどまらず、保護者を喪失すればその後の生存、生活と将来の希望も奪い去られる。

　子どもは全員が民間人であり、自らの意志によって実際の戦争に加担することも考えられない。疑いなく罪なき人間なのだ。

　しかし戦争を遂行する側は子どもを特別に保護することや攻撃対象から除くことに力を割こうとはしないし、できはしない。

　それどころかさまざまな形で子どもを戦争に利用してきた。世界では何らかの強制により戦闘員となった子どもが散見され、かつて日本でも「少国民」としての自覚を刷り込み、「早く大きくなって兵隊さんに」と戦意高揚をあおり、教育の場では敵国への憎悪と国家への忠誠をたたき込んだ。

　そのような事情は日本だけではなく、戦争や紛争、そのリスクを抱える世界各国で現在も同様に続いている。

Epilogue：Children of War

　No matter the reason or location, children are always the greatest victims of war, suffering death, injury, loss of caregivers, and stolen futures.

　As innocent civilians, children bear no responsibility for conflict, yet those waging war rarely protect them or exclude them from harm.

　Instead, children are often exploited. In wartime Japan, they were indoctrinated as "young citizens," taught loyalty to the state and hatred for enemies, and encouraged to aspire to military service.

　This exploitation of children is not unique to Japan. It continues today in many countries affected by war, conflict, or the threat of violence.

「安全への逃避」
"Flee to safety"

1965(昭和40)年9月6日、ベトナム中部ロクチュアン村で、危険から逃れようと必死で川を渡る2人の母親と3人の子ども。ベトナム戦争の悲惨さを捉えた写真は日本人カメラマンの沢田教一によって撮影され、ピュリツァー賞など多数受賞した。(UPI)

Two mothers and their three children fleeing across a river to escape US bombing, Loc Thuong Village, South Vietnam, September 6, 1965. The photograph, capturing the cruelty of the war in Vietnam, was taken by Japanese photographer Kyoichi Sawada who won numerous prizes for his work including a Pulitzer Prize. (UPI)

荷物担ぐ子ども
Children carrying their belongings

1951（昭和26）年1月、朝鮮戦争で北朝鮮側の攻撃から逃れるため、韓国・大邱操車場で、南行きの避難列車に乗り込もうと荷物を担いで歩く子どもたち。（ACME）

Children walk with their belongings to board an evacuation train at a shunting yard in Daegu, South Korea to escape attacks from the North during the Korean War, January 1951. (ACME)

食糧メーデーで訴える子ども
Children appealing for help on Food Mayday

1946（昭和21）年5月19日、敗戦後の食糧不足が深刻化する中、皇居前広場で開かれた食糧メーデー（飯米獲得人民大会）には25万人が参加、子どもたちは「オナカガペコペコ」と訴えた。

Amid a worsening food crisis after the war, 250,000 people attended the "Food Mayday" rally outside the Imperial Palace on May 19, 1946. This people's conference aimed to advocate for increased food supplies. Children voiced their hunger using the slogan "onaka ga pekopeko," which translates to "We are hungry."

食事を求める子ども
Children searching for food

2024(令和6)年3月5日、イスラエル軍とイスラム組織ハマスの戦闘が続くパレスチナ自治区ガザ南部ラファで食事を求める子どもたち。(ロイター)

Children seek food in Rafah, southern Gaza, Palestinian territories, as the war between the Israeli army and the Islamist group Hamas continues, March 5, 2024. (Reuters)

爆撃された建物と子ども
Demolished building and children

2022（令和4）年5月25日、ウクライナの首都キーウ（キエフ）近郊ボロディアンカの公園で遊ぶ子どもたち。
奥はロシア軍侵攻で爆撃され黒く焼け焦げた集合住宅。
Children play in a park in Borodyanka, the suburb of the Ukrainian capital Kyiv, May 25, 2022. The apartment complex in the background was burnt b ack by bombing in the wake of a Russian attack.

戦後80年関連年表

	月	世界の出来事	月	日本の出来事
1945(昭和20)年	5	ドイツ降伏	8.6	広島に原爆投下
	7	ポツダム宣言	8.9	長崎に原爆投下
	9	ハノイにベトナム民主共和国臨時政府樹立	8.14	御前会議でポツダム宣言受諾決定
	10	国際連合(国連)発足	8.15	終戦の玉音放送
			8.26	特殊慰安施設協会(RAA)設置
			8.30	マッカーサー連合国軍最高司令官が厚木飛行場に到着
			9.2	降伏文書調印
			10	東京・有楽町に連合国軍最高司令官総司令部(GHQ)設置
			12	衆院議員選挙法改正、労働組合法公布
			12	第1次農地改革
1946(昭和21)年	1	国連第1回総会	1	昭和天皇人間宣言
	7	米、ビキニ環礁で原爆実験	5	極東国際軍事裁判(東京裁判)開廷
	12	第1次インドシナ戦争	5	満州からの集団引き揚げ開始
			11.3	日本国憲法公布
			12	シベリア抑留者の引き揚げ開始
1947(昭和22)年	6	マーシャル・プラン発表	3	教育基本法・学校教育法公布
	8	パキスタン、インドが英領から独立	4	労働基準法・独占禁止法・地方自治法公布
	10	第1次カシミール戦争	5.3	日本国憲法施行
1948(昭和23)年	1	ビルマ連邦独立	1	帝銀事件
	5	イスラエル建国宣言(第1次中東戦争)	6	福井地震
	6	ソ連、ベルリン封鎖	11	東京裁判で25被告に有罪判決
	8	大韓民国建国	12	東京裁判の死刑判決7人に絞首刑執行
	9	朝鮮民主主義人民共和国建国		
1949(昭和24)年	4	北大西洋条約機構(NATO)発足	3	経済安定策「ドッジ・ライン」発表
	5	ドイツ連邦共和国(西独)建国	7〜8	人員整理などで混乱する国鉄めぐり下山事件、三鷹事件、松川事件発生
	9	ソ連、原爆保有を公表	11	湯川秀樹博士に日本人初のノーベル賞(物理学賞)
	10	中華人民共和国建国		
	10	ドイツ民主共和国(東独)建国		
1950(昭和25)年	6	朝鮮戦争	8	警察予備隊が発足
				朝鮮特需
1951(昭和26)年	11	米がネバダ砂漠で初の地上部隊参加による核実験実施	4	マッカーサー連合国軍最高司令官解任
			9	サンフランシスコ平和条約・日米安全保障条約調印(52年4月発効)
1952(昭和27)年	10	英、初の原爆実験	2	日米行政協定調印(のちの地位協定)
	11	米、初の水爆実験	4	海上警備隊設置
			4	日華平和条約調印
			10	警察予備隊を保安隊に改組
1953(昭和28)年	7	朝鮮戦争休戦協定調印	2	テレビ本放送開始
	8	ソ連、初の水爆実験	12	奄美群島返還
1954(昭和29)年	1	世界初の米原子力潜水艦ノーチラス進水	3	ビキニ水爆実験で第五福竜丸被ばく
	7	第1次インドシナ戦争でジュネーブ休戦協定成立	7	防衛庁、陸海空3自衛隊発足
	11	アルジェリア独立戦争(〜62年)		神武景気(〜57年)
1955(昭和30)年	5	西ドイツがNATO加盟	5	砂川闘争始まる
	5	東ドイツ含むソ連・東欧がワルシャワ条約機構結成	8	広島で第1回原水爆禁止世界大会
	10	サイゴンでベトナム共和国発足(南北対立激化)	12	原子力基本法公布
				三種の神器(冷蔵庫・洗濯機・白黒テレビ)が人気
1956(昭和31)年	7	エジプト、スエズ運河を国有化(第2次中東戦争へ)	5	水俣病の公式確認
			7	経済白書「もはや戦後ではない」と記述
			8	日本原水爆被害者団体協議会(被団協)結成
			10	日ソ共同宣言調印(ソ連と国交回復)
			12	国連加盟承認
1957(昭和32)年	8	ソ連、大陸間弾道ミサイル(ICBM)の実験成功と発表	1	南極観測隊、昭和基地開設
	10	ソ連、世界初の人工衛星スプートニク打ち上げ	8	東海村に「原子の火」、初の臨界実験成功
1958(昭和33)年	1	米、人工衛星エクスプローラー打ち上げ		岩戸景気(〜61年)
1959(昭和34)年	1	キューバ革命	3	砂川闘争で米軍駐留違憲の判決

年	月	世界の出来事	月	日本の出来事
1960(昭和35)年	2	仏、サハラで原爆実験	1	日米新安保条約、日米地位協定調印
		アフリカの年(17カ国が独立)	5	衆院、新安保条約強行採決、60年安保闘争激化
			12	池田勇人首相、12月に国民所得倍増化計画発表
1961(昭和36)年	8	東ドイツがベルリンの壁建設	2	「風流夢譚」事件
	9	第1回非同盟諸国首脳会議(25カ国)		
	9	西側20カ国で経済協力開発機構(OECD)発足		
1962(昭和37)年	2	米、サイゴンに軍事援助司令邹設置	8	原水禁世界大会分裂
	10	中印国境で紛争		
	10	キューバ危機		
1963(昭和38)年	8	米英ソ、部分的核実験禁止条約調印	8	第1回全国戦没者追悼式を東京・日比谷公会堂で開催
	11	ケネディ米大統領暗殺		
1964(昭和39)年	8	トンキン湾事件	4	海外観光渡航自由化
	10	中国、初の核実験	4	経済協力開発機構(OECD)に加盟
		キプロス紛争始まる	10	東京五輪
1965(昭和40)年	2	米、北爆開始(ベトナム戦争本格化)	2	原水禁結成
	9	第2次インド・パキスタン戦争	4	ベ平連、初の反戦デモ
			6	日韓基本条約調印
				いざなぎ景気(～70年)
1966(昭和41)年	5	中国、文化大革命始まる	10	ベトナム反戦統一スト
1967(昭和42)年	6	第3次中東戦争	12	佐藤栄作首相、非核三原則を表明
	6	中国、初の水爆実験		
	7	欧州共同体(EC)発足		
	8	東南アジア諸国連合(ASEAN)発足		
1968(昭和43)年	1	アラブ石油輸出国機構(OAPEC)発足	2	B52爆撃機が嘉手納基地に移駐
	8	仏、南太平洋で初の水爆実験	6	小笠原諸島返還
			10	新宿騒乱(ベトナム戦争に反対する過激派が駅構内占拠)
1969(昭和44)年	7	アポロ11号月面着陸	1	東大紛争、安田講堂占拠学生排除
			6	経済企画庁、68年の国民総生産(GNP)世界2位と発表
1970(昭和45)年	3	核拡散防止条約(NPT)発効、米ソ英仏中以外の核保有禁止	3	赤軍派学生が日航機よど号乗っ取り(日本初のハイジャック事件)
	4	米軍などカンボジアに侵攻、内戦へ	6	日米安保条約自動延長
			10	カメラマン沢田教一さん、カンボジアで銃撃され死亡
			11	三島由紀夫割腹自殺
1971(昭和46)年	8	米、金とドルの交換停止などドル防衛策(ドルショック)	7	環境庁発足
	12	第3次インド・パキスタン戦争		
1972(昭和47)年	2	ニクソン米大統領が訪中、米中共同声明	1	グアムで生き残り日本兵横井庄一さん発見
	5	米ソ、戦略兵器削減条約(SALT1)調印	2	札幌冬季五輪
	5	イスラエルのロッド空港で日本の過激派が銃乱射	5	沖縄返還
	9	パレスチナゲリラ、ミュンヘン五輪襲撃	9	日中国交正常化、日台断交
1973(昭和48)年	10	第4次中東戦争、第1次石油危機	12	政府、石油危機打開のため中東に特使派遣
1974(昭和49)年	5	インド、初の核実験	3	小野田寛郎元陸軍少尉をフィリピン・ルバング島で発見
			10	佐藤栄作元首相にノーベル平和賞
				戦後初のマイナス成長
1975(昭和50)年	4	レバノン内戦(～90年)	8	日本赤軍、クアラルンプールで米、スウェーデン両大使館占拠
	4	サイゴン陥落、ベトナム戦争終結		
	11	仏ランブイエで第1回先進国首脳会議(サミット)		
1976(昭和51)年	1	ポル・ポト派がカンボジア内戦に勝利、市民虐殺へ	4	横田基地騒音訴訟提訴
	4	天安門事件(第1次)	7	ロッキード事件で田中角栄元首相逮捕
1977(昭和52)年	11	エジプトのサダト大統領、イスラエル訪問	9	日本赤軍が日航機乗っ取り(ダッカ事件)
1978(昭和53)年	9	米、エジプト、イスラエル首脳会談	8	日中平和友好条約調印
1979(昭和54)年	1	米中国交正常化	6	先進国首脳会議(東京サミット)開催
	2	イラン革命、第2次石油危機		
	3	エジプト、イスラエル平和条約調印		
	3	米、スリーマイル原発事故		
	12	ソ連、アフガニスタンに侵攻(～89年)		

年	月	世界の出来事	月	日本の出来事
1980(昭和55)年	7	モスクワ五輪、日・米・西ドイツなど不参加		自動車生産台数が米を抜き世界一に
	9	イラン・イラク戦争(～88年)		
1981(昭和56)年	12	ポーランド戒厳令、自主管理労組「連帯」非合法化	3	中国残留孤児47人、初の正式来日
			4	貨物船日昇丸が東シナ海で米原潜と衝突、沈没
			5	ライシャワー元駐日大使が日米間に核持ち込みの口頭了解あったと発言
1982(昭和57)年	4	アルゼンチン軍、フォークランド諸島占領	6	米FBI、IBMへの産業スパイ容疑で日立社員ら逮捕
1983(昭和58)年		第2次スーダン内戦(～2005年)	1	中曽根康弘首相の「不沈空母」発言が米ワシントン・ポスト紙に掲載
1984(昭和59)年	12	香港返還後の一国二制度を盛り込んだ中英共同宣言調印		グリコ・森永事件
1985(昭和60)年	9	先進5カ国がドル高是正に合意(プラザ合意)	4	国有企業の民営化(NTT、JT)
			8	日航ジャンボ機が群馬県御巣鷹山に墜落
1986(昭和61)年	4	ソ連のチェルノブイリ原発事故		バブル経済始まる(～90年代初頭)
1987(昭和62)年	10	世界各国で株価大暴落(ブラックマンデー)	4	国鉄分割・民営化(JR)
	12	米ソ、中距離核戦力(INF)廃棄条約調印		
1988(昭和63)年	9	韓国でソウル五輪開催	6	リクルート事件発覚
1989(昭和64/平成元)年	6	天安門事件	1	昭和天皇が死去、皇太子明仁親王(現上皇)が即位、新元号「平成」
	11	ベルリンの壁崩壊	4	消費税(3%)スタート
	12	米ソ首脳会談、冷戦終結宣言		
1990(平成2)年	8	イラクがクウェート侵攻	1	「天皇の戦争責任」発言で本島等長崎市長が右翼団体幹部に撃たれ重傷
	10	東西ドイツ統一		
1991(平成3)年	1	多国籍軍がイラク侵攻(湾岸戦争)	1	湾岸戦争支援策として90億ドル支出決定
	6	ユーゴスラビアの解体・内戦	4	日ソ共同声明、北方領土4島を領土画定協議の対象とすることで合意
	7	米ソ、第1次戦略兵器削減条約(START1)調印	4	ペルシャ湾に掃海艇派遣
	12	ソ連解体、独立国家共同体(CIS)創設		
		ソマリア内戦(～現在)		
1992(平成4)年		アフガニスタン内戦(～2001年)、タリバンやアルカイダが台頭	6	国連平和維持活動(PKO)協力法成立
			9	カンボジアPKO派遣
1993(平成5)年	5	北朝鮮、日本海側に向け初のミサイル発射実験	5	カンボジアPKO文民警察官が銃撃され死亡
	9	イスラエルとパレスチナ解放機構(PLO)がパレスチナ暫定自治協定		
	11	欧州連合(EU)発足		
1994(平成6)年		第1次チェチェン紛争(～96年)	10	大江健三郎さん、ノーベル文学賞受賞
		ルワンダ内戦で約100万人虐殺される		
1995(平成7)年	5	中国が地下核実験	1	阪神大震災
	9	仏が地下核実験	3	オウム真理教による地下鉄サリン事件
			9	沖縄で米兵による少女暴行事件
1996(平成8)年	10	国連総会、包括的核実験禁止条約(CTBT)採択(2024年時点で未発効)	4	橋本龍太郎首相とモンデール米大使が沖縄の普天間飛行場返還など基地縮小で合意
			12	ペルーで日本人大使館公邸人質事件
1997(平成9)年	7	香港、英が中国に返還	4	消費税3%から5%に
	7	タイ通貨が暴落、アジア経済危機に発展	9	日米安全保障協議委員会(2プラス2)が日本周辺有事の新ガイドラインを決定
1998(平成10)年	5	インドが24年ぶりに核実験	2	長野冬季五輪開催
	5	パキスタンが初の核実験		
1999(平成11)年	3	対人地雷全面禁止条約発効	3	北朝鮮工作船2隻に自衛艦が初の海上警備行動
		第2次チェチェン紛争(～2009年)	5	日米新ガイドライン関連法成立
			8	国旗国歌法成立
			9	東海村核燃料施設で臨界事故
2000(平成12)年	6	韓国の金大中大統領が北朝鮮訪問、初の南北首脳会談	7	九州・沖縄サミット
2001(平成13)年	9	米中枢同時テロ	2	ハワイ・オアフ島沖で愛媛県の宇和島水産高の実習船えひめ丸に米原潜が衝突
	10	米英がテロ報復でアフガン空爆開始	10	テロ対策特別措置法成立
	12	米、ABM制限条約の一方的脱退通告	12	雅子皇太子妃(現皇后)が長女愛子さまを出産
2002(平成14)年	5	米口、戦略核弾頭数を最大2200個まで削減するモスクワ条約調印	3	自衛隊を東ティモールに派遣
	12	北朝鮮、核施設再稼働を発表	5	日韓共催サッカーW杯開催
			9	日朝首脳会談、日朝平壌宣言
			10	北朝鮮の拉致被害者5人帰国
				いざなみ景気(～08年)

年	月	出来事	月	出来事
2003(平成15)年	1	北朝鮮がNPT脱退宣言	4	日本郵政公社発足
	3	イラク戦争(～11年)	6	武力攻撃事態法など有事関連3法が成立
			7	自衛隊派遣するイラク復興支援特別措置法成立
			11	イラクで日本人外交官2人が銃撃され死亡
2004(平成16)年	3	スペイン・マドリードで列車同時爆破テロ	1	小泉純一郎首相がイラク南部サマワへの陸上自衛隊本隊の派遣決定
	6	イラク暫定政権発足	5	小泉首相が北朝鮮再訪問、拉致被害者の家族5人帰国
2005(平成17)年	7	英ロンドン中心部で同時爆破テロ	12	厚労省推計で人口が初めて減少
2006(平成18)年	6	イスラエル軍がガザ侵攻	7	陸自がイラクから撤収完了
	7	イスラエル軍がレバノン侵攻		
	10	北朝鮮が初の核実験		
2007(平成19)年	9	ミャンマー首都デモ取材中の長井健司さんが治安部隊の発砲で死亡	1	防衛省発足
2008(平成20)年	9	世界金融危機(リーマン・ショック)	1	新テロ対策特別措置法成立
	12	イスラエル、ガザ封鎖(ガザ紛争)	2	海上自衛隊がインド洋上で給油活動再開
2009(平成21)年	4	オバマ米大統領「核兵器のない世界」目指すプラハ演説	3	海上自衛隊がソマリア沖で護衛活動
		ギリシャ財政危機表面化		
2010(平成22)年	4	米ロ、新戦略兵器削減条約(新START)調印	9	尖閣諸島沖で中国漁船が海上保安庁の巡視船に衝突
2011(平成23)年	1	アラブ諸国で反政府運動「アラブの春」広がる(～12年)	3	東日本大震災、福島で原発事故
	3	シリア内戦、「イスラム国」(IS)介入	11	自衛隊の南スーダンへのPKO派遣を閣議決定
	5	米軍、国際テロ組織アルカイダの指導者ウサマ・ビンラディン殺害		
2012(平成24)年	4	北朝鮮、金正恩体制に	9	尖閣諸島を国有化
	5	ロシア、プーチンが4年ぶりに大統領再任		
	11	中国共産党、習近平体制に		
2013(平成25)年	1	アルジェリアのガス採掘施設を武装勢力が襲撃、日本人も10人死亡	12	国家安全保障会議発足
2014(平成26)年	2	ロシアでソチ冬季五輪	4	消費税5%から8%へ
	3	ロシア、ウクライナ南部のクリミア編入	7	集団的自衛権行使容認の政府見解を閣議決定
	9	米軍、シリアのIS拠点への空爆開始	12	特定秘密保護法施行
2015(平成27)年	1	パリの風刺週刊誌シャルリエブド襲撃	8	九州電力が川内原発1号機を再稼働
	7	米とキューバが54年ぶりに国交回復	9	集団的自衛権の行使を可能にする安全保障関連法が成立
	11	パリ中心部などで同時多発テロ		
2016(平成28)年	11	温暖化対策「パリ協定」発効	4	熊本地震
			5	オバマ米大統領が広島訪問
2017(平成29)年	9	北朝鮮が過去最大規模の核実験、水爆と主張	6	「テロ等準備罪」新設の改正組織犯罪処罰法成立
2018(平成30)年	5	米、イラン核合意離脱	6	成人年齢を18歳とする改正民法が成立
	6	初の米朝首脳会談	8	辺野古埋め立て承認撤回
2019(平成31/令和元)年	2	米、ロシアにINF廃棄条約破棄を通告、8月失効	5	徳仁親王即位、新元号「令和」
	6	香港で「逃亡犯条例」改正案撤回を求めて大規模デモ	10	消費税8%から10%に
			12	アフガニスタンで中村哲医師が武装集団に銃撃され死亡
2020(令和2)年	3	WHO、新型コロナで「パンデミック」表明	3	新型コロナウイルスで東京五輪・パラリンピックを1年延期
	6	香港で国家安全維持法施行		
	11	エチオピア紛争(～22年)		
	12	英国がEUを完全離脱		
2021(令和3)年	1	核兵器禁止条約発効、日本は不参加	6	イージス・アショア配備計画断念
	2	ミャンマーで軍事クーデター	7～9	東京五輪・パラリンピック無観客開催
	8	アフガンのタリバンが首都制圧、政権掌握		
2022(令和4)年	2	ロシア軍がウクライナに侵攻	3	ウクライナへ物的支援開始
			7	安倍晋三元首相が撃たれ死亡
			12	安全保障関連3文書を改定
2023(令和5)年	2	フィリピンの巡視船が、南沙諸島で中国艦船からレーザー照射受けたと発表	3	岸田文雄首相がウクライナを電撃訪問
	2	バイデン米大統領がウクライナを電撃訪問	5	G7広島サミット
	2	ロシア、新STARTの履行停止を表明	8	東京電力、福島第1原発から放射性物質含む処理水の海洋放出開始
	10	イスラム組織ハマスがイスラエル奇襲、人質約250人をガザに連れ去る		
2024(令和6)年	11	米大統領選でトランプ元大統領が勝利、25年1月就任へ	1	能登半島地震
			10	被団協がノーベル平和賞を受賞

※1945年から2024年11月までの出来事を掲載

寄稿

「日本の記憶」と「世界の戦争」

小熊　英二（歴史社会学者、慶応大教授）

　この写真展は「戦争と平和―80年の記憶―」と銘打たれ、5つのパートで構成されている。この写真展を観る人は、1930年代から1980年代までを対象とした前半と、1990年代以降を対象とした後半では、何かが変化していることに気づくはずだ。

　何が変化しているのか。もちろん前半は冷戦終結までが対象で、後半は冷戦終結以後が対象だ。前半はモノクロ写真が大半で、後半はカラー写真が大半だという相違もある。だが最大の相違は、前半は「日本の記憶」を扱っているのに対し、後半は「世界の戦争」を扱っていることだろう。

　もう少し具体的に述べよう。前半の写真は、敗戦直後と現代の日本各地を対比させるプロローグから始まる。第1章は「過信の果て」と題され、盧溝橋事件から三国同盟、真珠湾攻撃、学徒動員、学童疎開、特攻隊、原爆投下など、1937年から1945年までの「あの戦争」――歴史観に合意がないため「太平洋戦争」「大東亜戦争」「アジア太平洋戦争」「先の大戦」など呼称すら定まっていない「あの戦争」――の写真で構成されている（共同通信の前身である同盟通信の戦争責任にも言及している）。第2章は「『平和国家』の虚実」という題名のもと、敗戦と占領、帰還兵や戦争孤児、新憲法制定、再軍備をめぐる対立など、「あの戦争」の記憶が生々しかった時代の写真を中心としている。

　前半が扱っている1980年代までの日本は、「あの戦争」を経験した人びとが多くを占めていた。戦後生まれが人口の半数を超えたのは1976年である。敗戦時に10歳未満だった世代が首相になったのは1993年の細川護熙が初めてだった。それ以前の首相は、シベリア抑留から帰還した宇野宗佑、興亜院の官僚として内モンゴルに派遣されアヘン生産事業を担当させられた大平正芳など、思い出したくもなかっただろう戦争経験をした人が多い。

　1980年代までの日本は、戦争について直接的な記憶を持つ人びとが中心だった。そして当時の日本では、「あの戦争」のような事態は二度と引き起こしてはならないという合意が広く共有されていた。戦争は物質的な死や破壊だけでなく、精神的にも大きな傷痕を残していたからである。

　この時期の日本の人びとにとって、「あの戦争」はすべてにおける参照点であった。軍事も外交も、経済も政治も、「あの戦争」を基準として理解された。日米安保条約改定に反対が強かったのは、人びとが共産主義を支持していたからなどではなく、開戦時の大臣で戦争の責任者だった岸信介首相が改定を強行したためだった。ベトナム戦争に反対の世論が強かったのも、それが人びとの空襲や戦場での経験を想起させるものだったからである。

　この写真展の第2章までの写真が、「日本の記憶」を扱っていると形容したのは、上記のような意味においてである。たとえ朝鮮半島やベトナムでの戦争が被写体でも、そこでテーマとされているのは「あの戦争」の記憶なのだ。

　それに対し、後半にあたる第3章からエピローグまでの写真は、「世界の戦争」を扱っている。より正確にいえば、前半が「『あの戦争』とその記憶」が主題であるのに対し、後半はそのような記憶をもつ日本が「世界の戦争」にどう向きあったかが主題となっている。少なくとも、私にはそのようにみえる。

　くりかえしになるが、戦後日本は「あの戦争」の記憶のうえに築かれていた。軍事も外交も、経済も政治も、すべて「あの戦争」を参照点として理解された。自衛隊の海外派遣を禁じる国会決議が1954年に行われたのも、「あの戦争」の再来を防ぐ意図だった。

　しかし冷戦終結後は、そうした思考形態に再考を迫る事態があいついだ。湾岸戦争やイラク戦争は、「あの戦争」と必ずしも似ていなかった。カンボジアでの停戦監視活動、ソマリア沖での警戒監視活動などは、いっそう「あの戦争」との共通性が薄かった。

　こうした事態に自衛隊を海外派遣することは、「あの戦争」の再来につながるのか、そうではないのか。世論は割れ、国会でも激しい対立がおきた。それは、「あの戦争」の記憶を参照点として自国のアイデンティティを形成してきた戦後日本にとって、存在そのものが問われ

る事態だった。

　1990年代以後に人格形成した世代にとっては、上記のような議論が激しく行われたということ自体が不思議かもしれない。同時代においても、日本以外の国の人びとには理解しがたい議論だったかもしれない。しかしくりかえしになるが、それは戦後日本の存在そのものに関わる議論だった。

　そして「あの戦争」を経験した人びとが少数になり、その記憶が社会から薄れるにつれ、こうした議論そのものが下火になった。しかしだからといって、「あの戦争」に代わる新たな参照点が見出されたとは言いがたい。現代に至るも、「東京オリンピック」や「大阪万博」が折々の参照点として引っ張り出されている状態が、それを傍証している。

　写真展の第3章は「混迷の時代」と題され、自衛隊の海外派遣や災害支援活動、日米の共同軍事訓練、安保関連法への抗議活動、尖閣諸島沖の中国船、ウクライナやガザの事態などの写真が並列されている。そして最後のエピローグは、世界各地の戦時下における子どもたちの写真である。おそらく展示の意図は、「日本の戦争の記憶」を想起することで、「世界の戦争への想像力」を喚起しようというメッセージなのだろう。だが人によっては、写真の選択や配列が一貫性と説得力を欠き、展示そのものが「混迷」していると感じるかもしれない。

　だがそうだとしても、それは展示された写真の責任ではない。それを観る私たちが迷っていることの反映である。「あの戦争」からの80年は、戦争の傷痕と記憶から人々が解放されていく過程でもあった。その束縛から解放されたあと、私たちは「戦争と平和」について、日本について何を考えるか。この写真展は、その機会を私たちに与えてくれているのである。

小熊　英二（おぐま・えいじ）
1962年東京生まれ。1987年東京大農学部卒。岩波書店の雑誌「世界」編集部勤務などを経て、1998年、東京大大学院で学術博士号を取得。1997年に慶応大総合政策学部専任講師、助教を経て2007年から現職。膨大な文献調査に基づき民主主義やナショナリズムを緻密に考察し、96年「単一民族神話の起源」（新曜社）でサントリー学芸賞、2003年「〈民主〉と〈愛国〉」（新曜社）で毎日出版文化賞、15年「生きて帰ってきた男」（岩波新書）で小林秀雄賞など受賞多数。

寄稿

途切れなき戦争、なし崩しの「平和」

西崎　文子（歴史学者、東京大名誉教授）

　「恐ろしきもの走る」。1965年、日韓基本条約の国会での抜き打ち採決を目撃し、こう書いたのは大江健三郎である。冷戦構造がアジアに広まる中、中国や北朝鮮を排除したまま、独裁政権の支配する韓国との講和条約が締結されたのは日米安保の改定から5年後のことであった。安保改定時とは一変し、国民のあいだに無関心や無力感が漂う中、政府与党をなりふり構わず強行採決へと疾走させたものは何か。大江はそれを「時代という怪物」と捉え、その突進に嘔気をともなう恐怖を感じたのである。

　この「恐ろしきもの」は、戦後80年、日本人がおぼろげに感じながらも放置してきたものではなかったのか。われわれの多くは、作家の繊細な想像力を持ち合わせてはいない。目をそらせば、その姿は隠れてしまう。しかし、「時代という怪物」は、明らかにそこに存在し、アジアにおける途切れなき戦争の元凶となっていった。日本の敗戦から5年足らずで勃発した朝鮮戦争と、並行して深刻化したインドシナ戦争、そして、60年代に本格化する米国のベトナム介入。その中で、戦後日本は米軍の「庇護」と「重圧」とに絡みとられることになった。以後、日本が一瞬たりとも米国政府や米軍基地から自由であったことはない。そこに生じたのは、日本国憲法の非軍事的平和主義と、日米安保を基軸とする「現実路線」とのあいだの決定的な亀裂であった。憲法の平和主義は大きな矛盾を背負いこんだのである。

　その矛盾を鋭く見抜き、憲法の平和主義を積極的に生かす努力をしたのは、「恐ろしきもの」の矢面に立たされた地域、たとえば沖縄の人々であった。多くの日本人は、戦後経済復興の中で矛盾を忘れ去り、「現実路線」のもとで「平和」を謳歌する道を選んだが、太平洋戦争激戦の地沖縄でそれは許されなかった。戦後、日本から切り離されて米国施政下に入り、核兵器配備が進められた沖縄。本土復帰を目指す沖縄にとって、憲法は手に届かないものだからこそ、一層輝いて見えたのである。しかも、その状態は1972年の沖縄返還後も続いた。憲法の平和主義も「本土なみ」の夢も否定され、本土復帰してなお憲法の意味を問い続けなければならなかったのは、基地政策をめぐり選挙ごとに厳しい選択を迫られた沖縄の人々であった。

　この間、沖縄の苦悩を尻目に米国への依存を強める政府与党にとって、憲法はむしろ「足かせ」になっていった。それは、冷戦終焉後の状況に顕著である。湾岸戦争からアフガニスタン戦争、イラク戦争へと新たな戦争が勃発する中で、テロ対策特別措置法やイラク復興特別措置法の審議が行われた国会内外では、自衛隊の後方支援活動をめぐる激しい議論が巻き起こった。その焦点が、自衛隊の海外派遣に対する憲法9条の制約をどう解釈するかにあったのはいうまでもない。ただ、皮肉なことに、この間の議論が憲法の平和主義の積極的意義を問うよりも、9条が自衛隊に課す制約を軸に展開されたため、以後、憲法を日本の「国際貢献」に対する障害とみなす傾向が強まった。そして、今日では、「アジアにおける安全保障環境の悪化」を理由に軍事予算の拡大や日米の軍事一体化が進められているにもかかわらず、憲法論議は深まりを見せていない。憲法はなし崩し的に日米同盟の現実に道を譲り、その平和主義に込められた積極的意味は忘却されつつある。そればかりではない。憲法が不可視化された後には、新たな平和の概念が呼び込まれ、今や、平和は非戦や軍事力放棄ではなく、むしろ軍事力や核抑止論に依存する「力による平和」を意味するとの認識が跋扈している。

　しかし、私たちが進みえたのはこの道だけだったのだろうか。「時代という怪物」の前で震えるのではなく、より能動的に対応する道はなかったのだろうか。そうではないと教えてくれるのは、被爆者である。被爆体験のトラウマや放射線による健康被害への恐怖などをかかえて生きる被爆者は、この80年間、日々「恐ろしきもの」に対峙（たいじ）せざるをえなかった。彼らが自らの存在をかけて米国の核戦略に反対し、被爆者をないがしろにする政府を厳しく問い詰め、核兵器廃絶を訴え続けた理由はそこにある。このぶれのない姿勢こそが、われわれが戦後80年を振り返り、その先を考えるにあたっての道標にほかならない。

　われわれは、「憲法という肉体のすみずみにまでゆき

わたった動脈に、自分の心臓を直結させて、つねに新しい血をおくり、憲法を生きつづけさせておかねばならない」。大江健三郎がそう書いたのは、日韓基本条約成立から3年後の1968年、憲法制定から20年余りの頃であった。それからもうすぐ60年。幸いにも憲法は生き延びている。それは、「恐ろしきもの」をはねつけ、憲法を生かそうとする力が、思いのほか強かったことを意味するのかもしれない。そして今日、この力を維持し、強化できるかは、われわれにかかっている。ガザやウクライナで一般市民への殺戮が続けられ、強権政治がわがもの顔にふるまう時代を前にして、平和へのあらたな思索が求められている。

[参考文献]
大江健三郎「辱められた憲法とその『新生』」、「『恐ろしきもの』走る」
『大江健三郎同時代論集3　想像力と状況』（岩波書店、1981年）

西崎文子（にしざき・ふみこ）
1959年仙台市生まれ。東京大教養学部卒、イエール大大学院博士課程修了（歴史学）。成蹊大法学部助教授、同教授、東京大大学院教授を経て、現在は東京大名誉教授、成蹊大名誉教授。専門はアメリカ政治外交史。被団協の国際活動では通訳を務めるなど尽力。『アメリカ冷戦政策と国連、1945-1950』（東京大学出版会、1992）、『アメリカ外交の歴史的文脈』（岩波書店、2024）など著書多数。

定点観測者としての通信社 **戦争と平和** —80年の記憶—	A news agency as eyewitness **War and Peace** — 80 Years of Memories —
写真展 2025年1月11日（土）〜1月27日（月） 東京国際フォーラム ロビーギャラリー 主催 公益財団法人新聞通信調査会 協力 共同通信社 総合企画 河原仁志（公益財団法人新聞通信調査会） 写真選定 君波昭治、飯岡志郎（共同通信社）	**Exhibition** January 11 – 27, 2025 Tokyo International Forum (Lobby Gallery) Organized by Japan Press Research Institute In cooperation with Kyodo News Executive Producer Hitoshi Kawahara (Japan Press Research Institute) Photo Selection Board Shoji Kiminami, Shiro Iioka (Kyodo News)
写真集 発行日 2025年1月1日 編集 公益財団法人新聞通信調査会 共同通信社 執筆 小熊英二（歴史社会学者、慶応大教授） 西崎文子（歴史学者、東京大名誉教授） 飯岡志郎（共同通信社）＊コラム 君波昭治（共同通信社）＊写真説明 和文英訳 サマー・ウィラー ＊コラム インターナショナル ランゲージ アンド カルチャーセンター ＊写真説明 制作 erA 印刷 中央精版印刷株式会社 発行人 西沢 豊 発行所 公益財団法人新聞通信調査会 〒100-0011 東京都千代田区内幸町2-2-1 日本プレスセンタービル1階 電話03-3593-1081　https://www.chosakai.gr.jp ※本書のコピー、スキャン、デジタル化等無断転載は、著作権法上の例外を除き禁じられています。本書を代行業者等の第三者に依頼してスキャンやデジタル化することは、個人や家庭内の利用であっても著作権法違反となり、一切認められておりません。 ISBN978-4-907087-43-2 ©2025 公益財団法人新聞通信調査会／共同通信社	**Catalogue** Published on January 1, 2025 Edited by Japan Press Research Institute Kyodo News Contributors Eiji Oguma (Professor at the Keio University) Fumiko Nishizaki (Professor Emeritus at the University of Tokyo) Authors Shiro Iioka (Kyodo News) Column Shoji Kiminami (Kyodo News) Captions Translated and edited by Summer Wheeler Column ILCC Co., Ltd Captions Produced by erA Printed by Chuo Seihan Printing corporation Publisher Yutaka Nishizawa Published by Japan Press Research Institute All rights reserved. No part of the contents of this volume may be reproduced in any form whatsoever without the written permission of the publisher. Copyright © 2025 by Japan Press Research Institute, Kyodo News